Roadmap to Marketing SUCCESS

For Start-ups, Product Launches, or Career Changers

Maurice Hofmann

Workbook sections powered by
New York City Marketing Academy

Identifiers: LCCN 2020913035 | ISBN 9780578701721
| ISBN 9781735444109

Editor: Joann Sandone Reed
Print book design: HMDpublishing
Workbook provided by NYC Marketing Academy
Index and e-book: Walter Greulich
Illustrations: Christian Amouzou
Cover: Mira Falkenberg

Contents

Marketing and Communication Strategy . 112

Acknowledgements

To one nerd and slightly weird person to another – my wife, Saskia. I don't know what I would do without you in my life. It's not easy to find another person who loves to travel and loves nature as much as I do – especially when we can watch it through a window while sitting comfortably on a couch or in a car.

It's hard to find someone who likes the same weird people we both seem to attract like honey attracts bees. The tech stuff, your future projections of how we one day will live on this earth. Or our son, who is way too fond of certain places and is all over robots. Like, even toothbrushes are robots. Or sticks. Chairs. Vacuums. Anything. Everything.

The weirdness we share. The journeys we take. Expanding our minds one nutty idea at the time. Shoes, shirts, cars, projects... nothing ever shocks you. I love you and love we can share it all – your husband.

To my editor, Joann. Structuring me when it's needed. Making me feel good about my writing that is at best a Germerican hotchpotch before you sort it out and translate it for all to understand. For creative ideas and the openness for left turns.

And right turns.
And left.
Little more left.
No, right.
Let's start over.
Oh, I've written another book.
Are you ready?

Starting to work with you was easily the best idea I had with all of this. You made the curiosity I had about writing fun. So much so, that we have more, much more to work on.

Let's keep rocking this, my walking, cycling, running, and skiing friend.

PS: I still don't get how you like the cold.

Preface

What You Will Learn in Roadmap to Marketing Success

Based on my work with large multi-national firms, I believe there is a problem with current marketing practices. I've studied marketing and read scores of books on digital marketing, customer behavior, audience segmentation, and general marketing strategy. I get the sense all the so-called experts have forgotten about the basics. Countless friends who own start-ups ask me to recommend marketing books, but they inevitably return with much of the same questions they had before reading the books. Of course, they learned about their higher purpose in life and great marketing concepts, but not enough about steps one through ten. Business owners want to know

> You won't find a one-size-fits-all collection of marketing jargon here.

what they are supposed to do Monday morning when they turn on the lights. They wonder, what are the steps a talented software engineer, photographer, video producer, or fashion brand designer must take to reach their audience? Like them, you are reading this book because you want to know how to "do" marketing. Perhaps marketing isn't your primary profession, or everything you know about the subject came from that one university class many years ago. Or maybe those marketing textbooks are too theoretical for your taste.

That is where this book is different. It starts with what you should do Monday morning when you open the door and ends with what happens after you've launched your product or ran your first successful campaign.

This book covers the steps in a pragmatic and step-by-step fashion and will provide you with the core set of tools necessary to face your go-to-market campaign with the right strategic mindset. You'll get the operational know-how to turn your strategy into actionable items that will significantly increase your speed-to-market and reduce losses from trial and error. You won't find a one-size-fits-all collection of marketing jargon here. This book will guide you to the right marketing approach for you and your company, so you can pay the bills at the end of the month or deliver your project on time.

In the first part of the book, I will guide you and your team through a process that builds a strong working foundation and strategy. These planning steps range from re-thinking the position of your product and services, customer segmentation, all the way to how to set up your go-to-market operation that will serve as your market and business model.

Once you complete this strategy part, you will find actionable measures and the tools to get the job done.

With this book as your guide, you can focus on getting your brand or product to the market, one step at a time. You will find this and much more in the chapters that follow. Hopefully, at the end of this GTM adventure, you will appreciate the journey and be proud of the outcome.

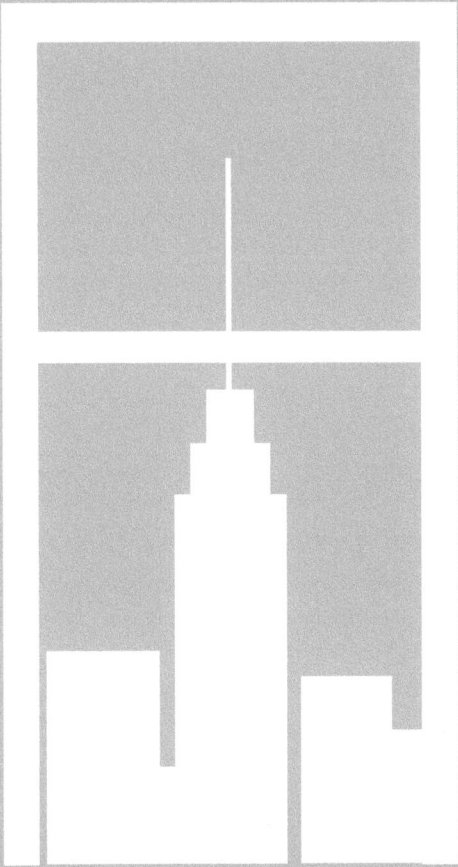

How and Why I Wrote Roadmap to Marketing Success

I wrote this book for you. I wrote it to guide your day-to-day marketing effort or help you create your grand marketing vision and strategy. However, I realize not everyone is in the same situation, and, like all of us, those situations evolve. So, I thought long and hard about making this book the best possible tool for a broad range of people interested in marketing who may be at various stages of their professional lives.

To do this, I drank a sip of my own "Research, research, research!" Kool-Aid and did my homework. Most importantly, I asked people I thought were the potential audience for this book, "What do you want from a marketing book?" They said, "We need actionable, day-to-day, applicable guidance. Tell us what to do that first Monday and what to keep doing to take us 100 Mondays later to our 101st."

Although that request is a tall order and one that may have to be supported by the NY Marketing Academy's accompanying website and Facebook Page, it led to inspiring discussions and ultimately influenced how I organized this book. To help you get the marketing job done, I laid out focused workstreams that guide you, step-by-step, from creating a strategy to planning and executing a launch campaign.

Please scan the QR code below to get to our website.

Please scan the QR code below to get to our Facebook Page.

The measures laid out apply to all industries and products, with minor adjustments. Many examples come from the software industry, where I worked for the last ten years. Product innovation, disruptive market entrees, and the start-up mentality culture of the software space are crying out for a book like this. Software is the foundation for some of the most successful and behavior-changing innovations of the past decades. Think Uber, Apple, Facebook, Google, Amazon, Netflix, or any of the top 10 apps you use daily. Software changes our lives every day.

This book is hands-on. If you want to get the work done, this is the book for you. I've studied many deep books and research papers on digital marketing and social media, which allows me to compare notes with other professionals and specialists. In Roadmap to Marketing Success and on our website, you will find links to helpful articles about the top tools to automate your messaging, get help for project management, and more.

I wrote Roadmap to Marketing Success so all you have to do is open it and get to work.

How to Work with this Book

The best way to work with this book is to think of it as a tool and daily resource that starts here, right now.

From the profiles described below and based on your current needs, decide which description fits you best. After each chapter, look for activities outlined for three different reader profiles. Follow the steps and action items or "workstreams" for your category.

At the end of each chapter, you'll also find links to resources from my website such as frameworks and templates, to help you with your particular workstream.

Reader Profiles for Workstreams

A. Product Launch

I geared this workstream for people who have little or no marketing experience. Follow workstream **A** for step-by-step guidance for launching your product.

A product launch requires the specific organizational and planning steps I've outlined and allows you to skip other activities to get your product to market quickly and efficiently. Sure, I could demand you work through every chapter the same way, but you may not have the time. Realistically, I know there are times when business owners need to get their product on the proverbial shelves quickly – digital or otherwise. For those who need to launch a product, its positioning, target audience, communication channels, and content marketing are more important than long-term strategy. The planning-focused, big picture tasks are indeed important, but not essential for a successful product launch.

If this sounds right for you, please follow workstream **A** at the end of each chapter.

B. Launch a Company-Wide Marketing Effort

Launching a company-wide marketing effort is a bit more challenging than a product launch. You need to consider every aspect of your company touched by a real marketing operation. For example, you must think about the marketing mix in addition to how team structure relates to sales or customer care, and then decide if you have resources, already allocated or not, for either. Your company-wide marketing strategy requires a more integrated approach than a product launch, which you might focus on one task that could be over in six months.

If the company-wide marketing description describes your situation, stream **B** is for you.

C. Learn Marketing Essentials and Processes

If you want to learn the essentials of marketing or polish your skills, all of Roadmap to Marketing Success is for you. You can work through the book from cover to cover or focus on a particular chapter. I suggest you read the whole book first, and then reread chapters as needed. Reading everything once will give you overall context. Once you have done that, you can go back and work on or clarify specific topics.

You may have inherited a role in marketing as so often happens in small companies ("Hey, can you take care of this marketing stuff?") or your current marketing role has expanded. It might be that you are changing careers. Or you are a marketing professional, but a few marketing skills on the mental bookshelf have collected a sprinkling of dust. Use this book as a feather duster for your skills.

If you want to learn all about marketing or need day-to-day general help, stream **C** is for you.

Be Interactive – with *Me*!

I arranged the chapters of this book to guide you through steps in the order that I use for all my customers. You can also get immediate advice and interactive help at our online academy and website. We have an entire eco-system available to make sure you find the answers you need when you need them. And of course, if you have more questions, feel free to reach out for more help. I am virtually always here.

Feel free to mix and match as you like, and don't forget to tell me about it. I want to hear what has worked best for you.

Here are my contact details:

@moreeze

@nyma

https://www.linkedin.com/in/maurice-hofmann/
https://nycmarketingacademy.com

Why Should You Listen to Me About Marketing?

From PsyOps to Marketing

Marketing simply happened to me. More precisely, I started young. I worked around communication and messaging, the foundations of marketing, as a 15-year-old in my hometown of Cologne, Germany. An aspiring dancer, I found my calling early by working with the media to get press coverage for my dance group. Granted, that is not the normal introduction for a future marketing professional. But, even as a kid, I was hooked on marketing. Right from the start, I was drawn to messaging, people, and what makes them tick. I still am.

As a young adult, I joined the "psychological operations" unit (PsyOps) in the German army where I served with the multinational forces of NATO in Bosnia. Here, in the middle of American, French, Russian, German, and Italian PsyOps, I learned what it meant to have the right and wrong message for your audience. I learned why you always have to start with your audience and back into your message.

PsyOps in Action

My life was so profoundly influenced by one day during my service with the German PsyOps, that I still remember the details like it was yesterday. I was on radio tour with my lieutenant. One of our tasks in Bosnia was to deliver tapes for the local radio stations to play. These tapes were primarily a mix of the latest songs, which the stations had no access to shortly after the war. The recordings also contained a sprinkling of brief messages about the current activities of the NATO forces, the upcoming first elections after the war, and general warnings and education about where mines were discovered or cleared.

> Here, in the middle of American, French, Russian, German, and Italian PsyOps, I learned what it meant to have the right and wrong message for your audience.

We had been on the road all day and already delivered tapes to several stations. At our last stop, I decided to stay downstairs and enjoy one of the rare moments of nice weather. Mind you, I was in the winter contingent during this, my second tour in Bosnia. They held the 1984 Winter Olympic Games there for a reason and I was tired of the clouds and cold that came with all that snow.

As I stood out there enjoying the afternoon sun, I noticed a man and his son approaching. Since I like kids and was nearly one myself — I was barely 21 at the time — I waved to the boy. He ran over and we chatted. We always kept some giveaways in our vehicles during these tours, so I thought I'd give the boy a treat. Since messaging was our mission and kids like comic books, we used Superman to help us warn them about the danger of hidden landmines.

In addition to candy and pens, we gave away 90,000 Superman comic books over a nine-month period.

I asked his father if it would be okay to give the boy a comic book. Surprised by my question, the man smiled and nodded. I must have triggered his curiosity because then the father asked me a few questions about who I was and what I was doing there. That's how we started a friendly conversation. He invited me to his coffee shop, pointing to a building not too far from where we stood, at the end of the block on the corner of two streets that forked to form a V-shaped intersection. I thanked him for his invitation and told him I had to wait for my lieutenant. When he returned, my lieutenant agreed we should accept the father's offer and visit his coffee shop.

That lieutenant was a funny guy. He did not speak a single word of English, French, or Spanish, but was as fluent as anyone could be in ancient Greek, Latin, and Hebrew. Obviously, those skills did not do him much good in 1997 Bosnia. That meant I translated English to German for him so he could take part in conversations with non-German speakers as we toured Bosnia together.

This created an interesting set-up a few minutes later when we sat down in the coffee house and my lieutenant quickly realized he could not actively participate in the conversation. Since he could not understand our conversation, he sat back and watched his corporal in action. I updated him occasionally and he took notes for the required contact report we both knew I would have to write when we returned to base.

Interest Yields Insights

Meanwhile, I was in the middle of a conversation about as sensitive topic as could be — religion. I was being vetted. The coffee shop owner told me he was an Iman who came to Bosnia to support his Muslim brothers beyond words and empty gestures — a strong, noteworthy statement about which I would write several pages later.

Although the Iman was willing to tell me a lot about himself, I could tell he first wanted to figure out who I was. I do not look like the average German, so I had to prove that I was indeed a German national and not an undercover American. Once I confirmed my identity, he asked me about my beliefs and how much I knew about my religion, Roman Catholic. There is clearly a belief that Catholics rank about as low as possible in the pantheon of followers of any religion in this regard. People seem to think Roman Catholics know nothing about their religion and care about it even less. Although there is some truth to that, I was fortunate to enjoy a private school education that exposed me to very tough, yet progressive teachings about religion and its meaning in today's world. I had never appreciated my early education more than during that discussion with the Iman.

I was relieved I could hold my own when challenged by this intelligent man. We talked about Islam, Christianity, and Judaism. We didn't use platitudes or make statements based on prejudice. Instead, we talked about similarities among religions and the responsibilities religious institutions have in the world. A discussion that was as relevant then as it is now, more than 20 years later.

In the middle of all this, my PsyOps training kicked in. I held my ground and was authentic, yet I left him room to establish himself, and he did the same. I was an interested and an active participant, but I made sure he knew I understood he held the superior position in this conversation. He was a very educated man and seemed to know more about my religion than most people. Indeed, he would have known more than me if it hadn't been for a former teacher, back in the day, Herr Degenhardt of the Liebfrauenschule in Cologne, Germany. Herr Degenhardt had piqued my interest just enough to make me want to learn more about Catholicism. He also challenged my classmates and me to look for meaning behind the words we read. He taught us written text is more complicated than the words that compose it.

Those lessons from my early school days resonated with my PsyOps training in which we learned to look for the root cause and motivation behind displayed behavior. Why did people act as they did at that moment and what was their intention? What caused the behavior and what would change it? Why turn left instead of right, and what influenced that split-second decision? Why buy this brand vs. the other? Or for this Iman, why did he invite me to his shop and what was the intention behind his questions and tests, and the loud and clear messages he gave me? He applauded me for my respectful behavior and marked it as, ". . . the first for any NATO soldier he had interacted with." The Iman explained other soldiers were rude and disrespectful. He said he enjoyed my authenticity and interest in his position. He also said he usually felt betrayed and ignored, as did his Muslim brothers. During this three-hour talk, we gathered more in-depth intelligence into the make-up of the Muslim community than we did in the entire four-month tour in Bosnia.

> That moment also taught me it does not matter how much you learn about your audience, your market; there is always much more you don't know.

Authentic Attention

I learned the value of active listening and the importance of being authentic and true to oneself that day. I carried that important lesson into my marketing life. I realized you only learn about your audience, your potential customers, if you listen to them in a non-judgmental way. Do not enter the conversation with the attitude that you already know more than they do. Be open and allow them to show their knowledge and share their insights. It may be more valuable than anything else you will learn. That moment also taught me it does not matter how much you learn about your audience, your market; there is always much more you don't know. For that reason alone, you must continue to reach out and listen for the insights they will share with you.

As for that 1997 moment in Bosnia, it had a happy ending. The winter sun had set by the time we were ready to leave the Iman's coffee shop and since we were not allowed to drive our car after dark, my lieutenant asked for protection. As we drove back to camp in our vehicle, now part of a safe three-car convoy, he looked over his notes and smiled at me. "That's a hell of a report you get to write," he said. "Be ready to tell that story once or twice." And so, I have.

Confident + Prepared = Upstart Success

After my time in the German PsyOps, I joined forces with friends and was a part owner of a marketing, TV production, and modeling agency. Here I realized I could apply all the strategies and tactics I learned with the army to the commercial field of marketing. We helped business owners, C-suite executives, and marketing "professionals," who wanted to reach an audience without knowing anything about it. Many of our clients didn't even know they needed those insights, and they lacked the tools to develop them. With a client network of 200 promoters in 50 German cities, we gave international companies deep insights into the culture and behavior of their target audiences. Our customers included all the big names in the sports fashion, music, movie, and video gaming industries. A few car brands rounded off our impressive upstart portfolio.

Our clever work attracted attention and Reebok invited us to pitch for the chance to manage their whole promotion budget. Since we were a confident bunch of sub-25-year-olds, we did not wear suits, nor did we even think it was a good idea to wear anything Reebok sold. Instead, we all wore Nike sneakers and t-shirts for a meeting with Reebok's head of marketing for Germany, Austria, and Switzerland. She was not amused. "You better give the best presentation of your life or I will kick you out of this building so hard you won't have to drive back home." She was a robust and tough woman, but it was obvious she was curious about us. She had heard about our successful marketing campaign that introduced K-Swiss to a non-tennis-playing audience and made them a cool brand all over Germany. Our efforts also drove legendary sales numbers for K-Swiss. It is safe to assume we had her attention the minute we walked in the door.

Research and More Research

Even though we were cocky, we were organized and prepared. Well before we showed up at Reebok in our inappropriate attire, we had sent 200 teams of young researchers throughout Germany to ask questions among their peers, pose as mystery buyers, and to survey sales staff in all the stores that sold Reebok at the time. All told, our teams collected first-hand intelligence that generated more than 100 presentation slides prepared by the brains of our crew, Nils, who was also a rising star at BCG Germany at the time. This became the basis for our campaign that turned around Reebok's poor reputation outside of the fitness community. I am happy to report even though that initial meeting with Reebok ran three-times the originally allotted time, we not only avoided the marketing officer's boot and drove home, but we also won Reebok's business for the next three years. Our friend in marketing, however, outfitted us in the newest Reebok/RBK gear and only half-jokingly made it clear she would not let us in a second time if we wore any other brand.

We won the account because the intelligence we gathered proved to Reebok they needed to better understand the target audience for their new brand. Our research showed a brand represented by edgy NBA star Allen Iverson wouldn't be successful when sold next to aerobic gear. We told Reebok they had to allow their desired audience to discover their product and experience Reebok anew.

> The foundation I built during my years in PsyOps was validated again: when given a chance, your target audience will give you all the intelligence you need to devise appropriate and successful marketing tactics.

We were confident this approach would work because of the reams of data our teams had compiled in preparation for the meeting. When our researchers went to basketball courts and urban lifestyle shops and showed the potential audience pictures of the RBK brand collection – Reebok's new sub-brand targeting a more urban audience – we got the best feedback and highest interest from the people who would one day sell the brand and from the kids who were supposed to buy it from them. Today, marketers have a much more scientific approach to their activities and call it "data-driven marketing." Back then, it came to us organically. We instinctively knew we weren't the same as the various audiences our customers wanted to reach, so we invested a lot of time learning about those markets before we defined the strategies and tactics for the proposed campaigns.

Listen and Learn

The foundation I built during my years in PsyOps was validated again: When given a chance, your target audience will give you all the intelligence you need to devise appropriate and successful marketing tactics. In Reebok's case, our first tactic was a basketball sales event. We launched the RBK brand with an opportunity for the potential audience to take part in something fun. We brought a basketball court, players, a DJ, and RBK gear into stores and allowed the audience to really experience what RBK was all about. The images of those events and how the kids felt while trying out the RBK gear boosted sales at every location for weeks. This tactic also launched RBK to an urban lifestyle audience who never would have considered Reebok otherwise.

During those early years, I learned the crucial lesson that my marketing work is not about fulfilling my dreams and pushing my concepts. I learned successful marketers must have a service mentality that is directed to achieve set objectives. Being of service, however, sometimes means to you must point to an uncomfortable truth that a client, or even your own company's management, does not appreciate. It is this kind of servant leadership that puts the benefit and satisfaction of the customer above everything. I had to learn to find the right balance.

At age 30 and after more than a decade, I moved on from the marketing agency and added an MBA to my credentials. For several years I helped other companies get started, turned around, and funded. I also moved from

Cologne, Germany to New York City. Well, just across the Hudson, which really is New Jersey.

Around the World to Home

One of my projects – TeamOpenOffice.org – landed me with Open-Xchange (OX) from Olpe, Germany. You've never heard of the Olpe? Don't worry, I lived 30 miles away from the town for 25 years and had never been there before I started working for Open-Xchange. Life is funny – I moved 4,000 miles away to find work with a company next door to my hometown.

At Open-Xchange, I had finally found another home, one for my accumulated knowledge and the opportunity to apply it. I worked on different projects and launched many initiatives, but none more important than the Customer Success Department, which I lead today.

Introduction

Marketing is a mix of groundwork, classic techniques, strategic processes, and if you are one of the chosen few, art and creative genius. Aside from Apple and Nike, we don't see a lot of marketing art or exceptional creativity from most companies. And this is all right. Not every marketing campaign can be a work of art that everyone wants to see and be part of just because it is cool. But we can do better.

When we review the research, we learn small to medium-sized businesses (SMEs) do a poor job creating and executing thorough marketing strategies[1.] This is particularly true of companies that are owner-managed or dominated by a strong sales focus. At these firms, marketing is often undertaken with a lack of focus due to limited resources — financial, labor, know-how, or patience to get the work done[2]. They undertake techniques like segmentation, customized messaging, strategic pricing, and customer relationship building haphazardly, or not at all[1].

Bake the Cake First

> Not every marketing campaign can be a work of art that everyone wants to see and be part of just because it is cool. But we can do better.

Marketing departments, SMEs, and agencies are all looking for a shortcut to the big idea. Most do not realize, there are thousands of hours of precise, nerve-racking work behind every bit of creative genius. Successful marketers work hard to plan and prepare each little element of their marketing campaigns. Any great campaign, even if it looks effortless, is preceded by months of detailed marketing research, analytics, process optimization, and exceptionally well-planned campaign strategies. Lest you think organized planning comes naturally to me just because I'm German, be assured, I work hard at it too.

Launch campaigns for worldwide products must follow specific steps before the genius works its magic. If the results lead to creative miracles, that is icing on the cake. But first, we must make sure there is a cake.

As a consultant on go-to-market (GTM) product introductions and brand launches for two decades, I have seen many cases where people thought the groundwork was boring and not important. They skipped details and thereby neglected crucial steps. Large marketing departments of even larger corporations could not plan a campaign from start to finish. Start-ups had no idea where to start or how to finish and lacked any direction in between. The introduction of digital marketing and all the opportunities and challenges it adds have only made the situation more complicated.

I take my clients back to the basics and Marketing 101 to help them refocus. I guide them through the necessary steps and groundwork. I show them how paying attention to the small steps, by working pixel by pixel, they create and complete the big picture. This way, we have a map to follow on the road to the campaign's launch, and suddenly the light at the end of the tunnel is not headlights of an oncoming train.

Each element of the map has a role. Market definition, segmentation of the target audience, the product's key selling points (KSPs), messaging, and finally the proper use of digital marketing channels — everything plays its part.

Commit to the Long Haul

Marketing always came easily to me because I never made it about myself. My time with the PsyOps taught me early on that the audience dictates your next step and you must know who they are. You may wish to influence their next step or alter their behavior to your benefit, but you will not change their actions, not even slightly, with a single campaign. And you certainly won't change their behavior until you have intelligence about your potential customers. Who are they?

The goal of our PsyOps engagements was to create sustainable change in our audiences' behavior, so we made the investment necessary to create long-term relationships. That is why I was part of multi-year engagements in Bosnia. Research shows it takes multiple stages to create relationships. In the digital or social media environment, researchers have identified five major phases of relationship building: disclosure, information, dissemination, interactivity, and involvement (Liu, J. H., North, M., & Li, C., 2017). There are no shortcuts here. If you want your audience to change their view of you, your product, and what it is you want them to do — subscribe to your service or buy your product — you must invest in building the relationship. It is not over though; the human tendency to wonder, "What have you done for me lately?" means you must reaffirm this hard-won relationship with every interaction and experience.

Let's not jump ahead, however, there is a time for everything, and we need to start at the beginning: What is your mission? For example, sometimes my PsyOps training concentrated on influencing short-term decisions. Go left instead of right. Listen before you start shooting again. In the marketing space, you need to distinguish if you are on a long-term mission or working on a seasonal sales campaign. Just as with PsyOps, there are engagements designed to improve the overall impression or brand, and there are missions that just aim at making the enemy stop shooting or the customer buy a new product. Knowing which is important at what moment is the fun part.

Data Drives Success

In this day and age, no product is launched without data-driven decisions. Even Apple, under Steve Jobs' tenure, someone who openly said, "Customers don't know what they want." (Forbes, 2011), used an enormous amount of intelligence collected by him and his state-of-the-art designers. The average business that aspires to Apple's success must commit a substantial amount of resources to market research to gather this wealth of data. (Un)fortunately, most of us are not Steve Jobs nor do we have access to his staff. We, therefore, must do this groundwork ourselves. However, even leaders at large firms like United Airlines, Bank of America, and Mercedes-Benz routinely seek a few minutes of time to answer their survey questions when they contact me, a customer and user, for market research and intelligence gathering.

Know When to Ask for Help

No matter the industry or size of the firm, it is a sign of professionalism to know what you do not know and to consult experts in current best practices. Some of the biggest and most successful companies in the world know when to ask for help. One of my clients is GoDaddy, the world's largest domain name registrar and host of cloud platforms for independent ventures. I am working with this huge company, who clearly knows marketing, because they want to know Open-Xchange's current tips and best practices to launch OX products. In fact, they are proudly receptive to learning the latest tactics and techniques to improve their business. They know the world of marketing changes quickly and fortune favors the open-minded. Their website proclaims, "We live by the same principles as any successful startup: hustle, adapt, listen. Repeat." Does that sound familiar?

When we look at the landscape of the greater marketing arena, we find the best marketers in any business use an intelligence-gathering and a data-driven approach. Successful marketing is based on the intelligence you have about your audience. The methods of tactical PsyOp units in 1997 Bosnia and professional marketing departments in 2018 are quite similar.

My work with PsyOps taught me it is key to take time and look at the person across from you, engage with them without prejudice and keep an open mind, but keep your goals in sight. In the world of marketing, you only learn about your

> Successful marketing, now more than ever, is based on the intelligence you have about your audience.

audience, your potential customers, if you are able and willing to listen to them in a non-judgmental way. Do not enter the conversation with an attitude you already know more than they do. Be open and allow the person you're trying to persuade to demonstrate their knowledge and share their insights. It may be more valuable than anything you learn. My PsyOps experience taught me, no matter how much you think you know about your audience, there is always something you do not know.

Look at your audience. Put them at the center of your efforts and learn about their motivations and needs. What keeps them up at night? How does basic human behavior affect their actions? Successful marketing, in 2021, more than ever, is based on the intelligence you have about your audience. You must have an intrinsic interest in your audience to find the right message and trigger the desired reaction.

Customers are also more empowered than ever thanks to the digital revolution of the past two decades, so a customer-centric approach is no longer a nice-to-have tactic, it is elementary. You need to know your customers, allow them to find you, and listen to what they tell you. Customer engagement and the success your customers have with your product will make or break your business. Customers are human, they will tell their peers from around the corner, or around the globe, about their experience with your firm and product. Today's "word-of-mouth marketing" is human nature accelerated by the digital revolution.

Go-to-Market (GTM) vs. Corporate Marketing

In this book, I will get you started with marketing. Whether you need a go-to-market campaign for a product or you're about to launch your brand, getting started is often the hardest part. Owners and marketing officials, especially those at young companies, often feel overwhelmed by the number and volume of things they think they must do. They lose sight of the easiest and most basic steps. It is those basics that differentiate a go-to-market campaign from the much bigger task of creating a corporate marketing strategy.

Corporate marketing includes areas like branding and corporate identity (CI), brand building, sales strategies, product marketing, the overall and financial business case for a company and its products and, finally, how to go to market (GTM). The GTM process is a microcosm of everything corporate marketing does on the operational side. It breaks down the process into the essence of who wants to supply what to whom, and how?

A GTM campaign has the luxury to focus on a single campaign with a specific timeline. When a company launches a brand or a product with a GTM campaign, it can seem like this launch defines the firm, and that may be true. Successful corporate marketing, however, needs to have a mid- and long-term strategy in place that exceeds the go-to-market campaign. In fact, the GTM campaign must adhere to standards set forth by corporate marketing such as company culture, corporate objectives, and the general positioning of the company to list a few, and not necessarily in that order.

Which Comes First?

If you are creating the GTM for your main brand and its product line(s), the process and steps laid out in this book can be a good opportunity to feed into and grow your corporate marketing strategy. Sometimes time is sparse, and you need to get your product on the proverbial shelf to start generating revenue, so you can pay the bills or, if you are one of the lucky ones, to show your investors progress. Even when you feel rushed, set aside a little time to review your course of action and make sure you align it with your original idea. You can modify and adjust those ideas, but it should be a conscious decision that lets you, your team, your company and, at the end of the day, your brand, grow in a direction you can stand behind and be proud of. Certainly, that does not mean things won't change in a month, a year, or ten years. As Heraclitus of Ephesus said around 500 BCE, there is no constant in life but change. The biggest companies in the world know they must be able to change quickly to keep pace. The inevitability of change aside, take the time to consider your overall corporate strategy and ethos. You don't want to regret a decision because it did not reflect the spirit, ethics, and culture of your company. Those are tough to regain once lost.

A corporate marketing strategy can provide the foundation for a GTM campaign. The reverse is also possible and is the more realistic scenario in this fast-moving and agile world.

With this book, you can focus on getting your brand or product to the market, one step at a time. Hopefully, at the end of this GTM adventure, you will appreciate the journey and be proud of the results.

I will guide you, step-by-step, from creating your strategy to the planning and execution of a launch campaign. The measures laid out in this book apply to all industries and products, with minor adjustments in the choice of channels. Many of my examples will come from the software industry, where I have worked for the last 10 years. It is also an environment in which product innovation, disruptive market entrees, and a culture of start-up mentality cry out for a book like this. Software has become the foundation for the most successful and behavior-changing innovations of the past decades. Think Uber, Apple, Facebook, Google, Amazon, Netflix, or any of the top 10 apps you use daily. Software changes our lives every day.

This book is hands-on. If you want to get the work done, this is the book for you. I've studied scores of in-depth books and research papers on digital marketing and social media which allows me to compare notes with other professionals and specialists. In Roadmap to Marketing Success, and on the accompanying NY Marketing Academy website, you will find links to informative articles that will introduce you to top tools to automate your messaging, get help for project management, and more.

Please scan the QR code below to get to our website.

This book starts the moment work needs to get done and goals achieved. You can also get immediate advice and active help at our online academy and website. We have an entire eco-system available to make sure you find the answers you need when you need them.

Be Interactive – with *Me*!

I arranged the chapters of this book to guide you through those basic steps in the order I use for my customers. Feel free to mix and match as you like, and don't forget to tell me about it. I am more than curious to hear what has worked best for you.

Reach out!

Contact details:

Website: https://nycmarketingacademy.com

On Twitter: https://twitter.com/NYMKTAC

@nymktac – NY Marketing Academy account

Or https://twitter.com/moreeze   @moreeze – personal account

On Linkedin: https://www.linkedin.com/in/mauricehofmann/

On Instagram: https://www.instagram.com/NYMKTAC/

On Facebook: https://www.facebook.com/NYMKTAC

I look forward to taking this journey with you. Now let's start the ride.

Workbook

📖 Topic   Why are you reading this book?

Ask yourself the question, "What do I want to accomplish?" Choose an answer from one of the three objectives listed as Workstreams A, B,C. After each chapter, look for activities outlined for the three different reader profiles. Follow the steps and action items or "workstreams" for your category.

📋 Workstream

A	B	C
Launch a product	Launch a compny -wide marketing	Learn marketing essentials and

🖊 Key take aways

☑️ To Do

-
-
-
-
-
-
-
-

Challenges for Marketers in 2021

Before you devise a go-to-market strategy for a company or product, you need to consider the perspective of your potential customer. Right now, your customer has no idea that your company or your product exists, or why she should be interested in buying your product. Even worse, a single encounter with you or your marketing messages posted on the various channels will not put your product at top of the list of things she wants to buy. In today's world, your potential customer encounters hundreds of marketing messages per day. She'll actively register some of them, others will just be subliminal or subconscious noise. This means you must break through the noise. You must move your customer from a state of passive awareness to direct consideration, and finally, to make the purchase.

Empowered Consumers

> These customizable news aggregation channels like RSS feeds, social networks, or web portals allow users to escape traditional information outlets altogether.

Today's consumers are moving targets who use multiple devices throughout their day. It is not the 1950s where you had three or four outlets to worry about: newspapers, radio, billboards, and TV in the evening. Users today are also more autonomous in how they choose to consume information. Almost everybody chooses their own media and information sources, so they consume very targeted information. These customizable news aggregation channels like RSS feeds, social networks, or web portals allow users to escape traditional information outlets altogether. And, more importantly, their Artificial Intelligence (AI) engines drive added sources of similar information to the top of users' streams and search results. This further precludes your new and different information from reaching your desired audience.

So how do you reach your audience and make sure they not only passively come across your messages, but actively register the information and translate it into action? The answer to this is as easy as it is complicated: Make sure you are where your customers are and that you relay a message that interests them and makes them want to know more. When they learn more, you've hopefully made them interested enough to buy your product. Then, to make the situation even more challenging, the customer must also use your product and upgrade to the premium, and eventually newer versions. Or, if you're not in the app or software industries, you'll want your first-time customer to buy something from a new collection or version of your product. This basic rule applies to all services and products on earth: Satisfied and returning customers are the key to success.

But first things first. Let's get the message to the customer first and then worry about how you make her an active user and returning customer.

You do not win the war for a customer in a single battle. It is a constant struggle during which you must prove to the customer that it is worth their effort, time, and money to know, remember, consider, and finally, buy a product from you.

Channels: All Streams Flow to Your Message

You need to create an integrated marketing strategy that gives the user a mix of inbound and outbound channels which the user can choose at her convenience.

Inbound channels allow a researching customer to find the information you have provided by searching for product or brand name based on her needs, or because she overheard something from friends, family, or peers, offline or online. Information is available on demand to your audience. They decide when and how they want to consume it.

Outbound channels, on the other hand, seek out your potential customer and actively put your information in front of her. The right mix of both will determine the success of your campaign. A good balance between inbound and outbound, or "push & pull," is important. On your outbound channels, you "pull" and then channel your audience to your inbound resources. There you can present more detailed information than you can on outbound channels. Messages you "push out" must be quick and catchy.

Data Drives Success

Next, you have to build those messages for your targeted audience. This is when it is crucial to know as much as possible about your customer. As my saying goes, "data drives success." If your target audience is this blurred mass of unknowns, you won't able be to find the right message for the right time and at the right place to catch their attention. For example, it does not make sense to place your advertising banners in a soccer stadium in Spain if your customer prefers to watch American fashion shows online.

Privacy

You'll also gather information about your customers and use it to your marketing advantage. Remember however, you want to create value for your customers and not exploit the intelligence gathered about them. In a healthy and sustainable relationship, it is your responsibility to protect your customers and their privacy.

The European Union (EU) General Data Protection Regulation (GDPR) Impacts Businesses Worldwide

Data security and privacy is the latest challenging topic for all of us. Although the U.S. still lags, recent data breaches and the revelations revealed by Mark Zuckerberg's statements before the U.S. Congress, have pushed other regions of the world to act. At the forefront of this movement is the European Union's **G**eneral **D**ata **P**rotection **R**egulation (GDPR). This new law "will fundamentally reshape the way in which data is handled across every sector, from healthcare to banking and beyond.". The GDPR requires businesses and all players in the digital world – big or small – to expressly seek permission from customers, users, page visitors, newsletter subscribers, or social media audiences to use their data to contact them and to store their data for any purpose. The regulation also goes a step further, and mandates mechanisms are in place to confirm the user gave the initial permission, called "double opt-in." Although this sounds like doom and gloom and something you need legal counsel to manage, it is an opportunity for business owners from SoHo (small office/home office), to enterprises, or corporations, who do their jobs right.

The GDPR Levels the Playing Field

Thanks to the GDPR, businesses will no longer be able to short-cut the lead process by buying stolen lists of users or businesses from international data sets. Just ask Marriot (5 million data sets), My FitnessPal (150 million data sets), Quora (100 million data sets), or Facebook (29 million data sets) what happened when hackers stole their data.

The U.S. will eventually follow suit, one way or the other, perhaps for no other reason than they must. These EU regulations apply to all companies that process personal data of subjects who live in the EU, regardless of the company's location. We expect all companies to adopt this standard soon. If they don't, their business practices will be too difficult and cumbersome.

As noted in the PrivSec report, *How GDPR is shaping global data protection,*

"Thanks in part to the Facebook/Cambridge Analytica saga, and before that the Snowden leaks, the world is waking up to the dangers of how modern technology can erode our privacy. GDPR has set a high benchmark, citizens around the world are calling for more protection, and some countries are following."

Marketers must quickly adjust to these regulations because there is no way around them. Here are some resources that further explain the impact of GDPR and help you come to terms with the law:

- EU GDPR.org: https://eugdpr.org/

- Hubspot's GDPR check list: https://www.hubspot.com/data-privacy/gdpr-checklist

- Compliance Junction: GDPR for Small Businesses: A Beginner's Guide: https://www.compliancejunction.com/gdpr-for-small-business/

Disclaimer: This is not legal advice. You should consult legal counsel to make sure you achieve full compliance with the GDPR or similar regulations.

Key take aways

To Do

NYMA

A Few Words About Plans

Plans are important. It is as simple as that. As Antoine de Saint-Exupéry said, "A goal without a plan is just a wish." You will read a lot about plans of all shapes and sizes in this book. I create plans for different steps of the GTM process, but I also make plans for corporate marketing. A plan gives you a safety net for when the going gets tough or hectic. When you have a solid plan in place you can open that document, take a deep breath, and consult your past self. What were your thoughts, ideas, and goals? What strategies and tactics did you plan to use to achieve your goals? It is helpful to remember what your original aspirations were. This doesn't mean what you wrote in the past is set in stone. Quite the contrary; revisiting past plans allows you to measure your growth and adjust course to reflect that growth.

Types of Plans

I distinguish between two kinds of plans, strategic or projecting plans, and transactional plans.

Strategic Plans

Business and marketing plans belong to the former group of plans that outline a strategy and supply a prognosis for future development and activities. These are the plans that are most likely to be revised over time. Even though they are subject to change, these long-term plans give you the guidance and structure to calmly go about your daily business. When things get busy, a good plan keeps you from running around like a chicken without a head. These types of plans help you define your business objectives and identify the grand steps it will take to achieve milestones and goals. They contain a lot of information that not only helps you along the way, but also makes it easier for internal and external stakeholders to understand your goals and decide if they want to join, finance, or support your efforts.

Business Plans

Business plans are funny things because they are often outdated by the time you finish writing them. Your business plan, however, starts a process of deep reflection that is healthy, particularly when you first begin your business. The process forces you to take an outsider's perspective on your company. Of course, both marketing and business plans contain important financial information. Even though it sometimes feels like that financial information may as well be written in sand, for an outsider, it is an insight into your mind. Everyone gets very honest about their ambitions once they set numbers and milestones for them.

The business plan focusses on the projected development of your company. In addition to the marketing plan, it contains elements that highlight how you want to produce or develop your product, how you intend to stay relevant, financial projections, and how you will grow your company and hire the right people. The business plan is the backbone of your company and, as I mentioned before, it is the one you are most likely to change often as you, your company, and your goals evolve.

> Everyone gets very honest about their ambitions once they set numbers and milestones for them.

Marketing Plans

Another long-term or strategic type of plan, the marketing plan, is narrower in scope. Marketing plans outline advertising and marketing activities designed to sell (or license) a product or service. A marketing plan contains product marketing specific information like packaging and pricing, outlets you'll use to sell your product, and your advertising strategy. It should also have and highlight a deep knowledge of your audience. This is where you must address how you will gather all the valuable customer intelligence it takes to realize your sales projections. Although a business plan is important to help you find investors or win capital, investors or financiers also want to see annual marketing plans. With marketing plans, they can track not only the results of your past year but also get a good understanding of your chance for success. Companies with the highest values have the best profit to revenue ratio. But companies that also supply the most reliable financial prognosis, usually measured by marketing plans and reports, are investor favorites. There is nothing scarier to an investor than something they cannot understand or predict. A well-written and substantial marketing plan helps them do both.

Transactional Plans

Finally, there are what I like to call, the transactional plans. In transactional plans, you lay out a course of action. This type of plan outlines the particulars and the sequence of activities described in the marketing plan. Think of the go-to-market plan or launch plan as a construction plan and road map. Everything you want to do should be described in detail, so the combined sequence of actions takes you down the road to your goal.

Let's say you want to promote your product with a video on your web site. In that case, there are three major parts of the process you have to plan.

Create the web site or landing page that will host the video. Supply more details such as the steps you want the user to take while on the site: watch the video and follow the call-to-action. What do you want the user to do next? Buy something, subscribe to a newsletter? Any good web site also needs copy, graphics, a designer, and programmer, and they all must work coordinated with the team that creates the video and promotions.

Produce the video. You will need to write a script that includes the message and content of the video and describes layouts for the look and feel of the piece. If the video has a voice-over, that needs to be recorded as well. The voice-over will determine the duration and rhythm of the video. You'll test a draft version of the video with the target audience to make sure the message you want to relay is received. You repeat that process a few times until the tests for the video come back, "good enough." For me, good enough is when you reach 80% approval since it is too tough to reach 100% with a reasonable amount of effort. I always encourage my clients to regard collateral such as a video as a "living" object that evolves over time in response to feedback or the need to change the message.

Plan promotional activities that channel the audience to your web site and guides them to take the desired action.

This brief description of what is a far more complicated process highlights how the various elements of a simple task, like launching a new product video, depend on each other. I produce such videos and landing pages for large companies from across the globe. For larger companies, I commonly include the following teams in the process:

product management, product marketing, market research, brand, communications, legal, and customer care.

The bigger the team, the more complicated it is to organize and harmonize. This is where transactional plans prove their value to the project. Yes, even the production of a small video is a project that must be managed. This leads us to another name for the go-to-market or launch plan: the project plan.

In summary, plans document and communicate intentions, objectives, and the processes used to realize the former. The type of plan used depends on the situation. It is common for one plan to include two or three other smaller or more focused plans.

📖 Topic   A few words about plans

📄 Workstream

A

Create a go-to- market plan.

▶ What product do I want to launch?

▶ How do you want to launch the product?

▶ Stay tuned and keep reading for step-by-step guidance.

B

Create a business plan.

▶ What problem does my company or product solve? For whom?

▶ Create a detailed description of your company's solution(s) and target market(s).

C

Create a marketing plan.

▶ Create a marketing plan for a sample company.

✎ Key take aways

☑ To Do

NYMA

Get Started: Create a Go-to-Market (GTM) Campaign

A Quick Overview

Crafting a go-to-market (GTM) campaign can be a confusing process, but it is easier when you follow some clear and well-defined steps which you'll put together with the customer at the center of it all. Your customers will decide if they like what you put in front of them. Since they will determine your success, you must look at the product, its features, and benefits in the context of your audience, the customer. Then you'll create packaging and pricing that is attractive to your identified customers.

Of course, what's happening on the competitive landscape matters too. If you are a pioneer in your market, congratulations, you just need to focus on your potential customers. If you want to enter an existing or competitive market, however, it is critical to distinguish your brand or product from the competition. Your audience wants reasons for why they should choose your product or brand over that of your competitor.

Now that you know what you want to sell and to whom, and at which price, you can start thinking about messaging, preferred channels, and then, finally map out steps and timelines.

Before you start mapping, however, here are some key points to remember on the way.

> The best-practices of marketing all have an iterative process at their core.

Take your time — this is a process you cannot complete in five minutes. This book, however, offers you a very pragmatic and hands-on way to achieve your goals. Allow yourself to get there on your own time.

There is no need to be perfect — you will never be perfect. None of us will, that is a fact. But you can strive to be better today than you were yesterday or the day before. The best-practices of marketing all have an iterative process at their core. Do something. Test it. Learn from the tests. Improve what you've done, test it again, and so on. You'll be better tomorrow because of the work you do today.

First Things First

What is your product or service?

There are a couple of ways to begin your go-to-market process. All of them start with two key factors you simply cannot forget:

- Your customer

- Your product/service

Although all your marketing efforts should center around your customer, my clients often have a product before we identify their customers.

With that in mind, let's start with your product or service:

- What is it you do?

- What product do you want to sell?

If you cannot answer those questions right now, you may want to skip ahead to the Communication Exercise in Chapter 10. It will help you formulate your vision and mission. It will also encourage you to sort out your thoughts and just might challenge everything you think you know about yourself, your company, and your product. By the time you are done, you will know what your product or service is all about.

It is critical to be crystal clear when you define your product or service. You will not distinguish yourself from your competition if you try to be all things to all people.

Who is your product for?

As I've mentioned, and you will likely tire of hearing it, in-depth knowledge about your target audience is key. This means you must know who they are as a type, what their needs are, where to find them, and the best way to present your product or service to them.

If you want to have a compelling offer and top-notch customer service, you must strive to know as much about your customers as possible. In what is a never-ending process, you must constantly improve your understanding of your customers, your market, and your competition

Don't panic, it is okay if you don't have a clear picture of your customer at this point. We will get you there, but start thinking about it now.

Which problems does your product or service solve for your customers?

To match your product with the right customers, you need to know what problem your product or service solves, and the needs it meets. In short, how will your brainchild help your customers achieve their goals and reach their desired outcomes? This, again, goes back to knowing as much as you can about your customers, but it also requires another step and question: How would your product fill your customers' needs right now? Answer this question and you can position your product or service right in the middle of your customers' path to solving their problem.

How Does Your Customer Learn about Your Product/Service?

We all have our preferred approach to learning about a product or service before we buy or sign up for it. For example, it is particularly important for my wife to find recommendations from multiple sources about a new store, restaurant, or even an online course. The more reviews she can find, the better. Of course, they must be four stars or better (in a five-star system). Others might be a bit more explorative and prefer to learn about something first-hand. These customers would be perfect for a trial period or you can channel them to a local retail location.

You should consider your potential customers' research habits when you craft your message and set up the infrastructure that delivers the search results.

Where Do You Reach Your Customers?

This can be a tough question because you must consider more than your customers' physical location. These days, your customers can be anywhere around the globe and there are multiple ways to reach someone, so there is no universally best location from which to reach out. You'll also want to determine the medium your customers use to search for and consume product information, suggestions, and reviews. You need insight into your customers' state of mind; are they open to thinking and talking about your product? You should have some initial ideas about the answers to these questions when you start your go-to-market plan. These are important and fluid tidbits of customer intelligence, so expect to update them constantly.

What is Your Winning Message?

You have gathered intelligence about your target audience. Now you must collate, consolidate, and translate it into an appealing message. This is where you correlate your product know-how and customer insights; combine and analyze that data to create the right message to achieve your objectives. Then create a few, but strong key selling propositions (KSPs) to use across your channels to reach most of your desired target audience. Start with three winning messages that tell your audience why testing, licensing, or buying your product is in their best interest.

How to position yourself, your company, and your product?

While the earlier questions focused on you (product, service, company) and your customers, it is time to take a broader perspective. It is extremely rare in 2018 to have a unique and pioneering product. It is more likely you will find competitors in the market who, in some way, do the same thing or have the same product as you. Ask yourself, how are you alike and how you are different in what you do, how you do it, and who you do it for? Distinguishing factors are quality, quantity, price, market segment, region, time, industry, and business model. This is not a complete list. There are many others and it is up to you to research and determine your distinguishing factors.

I know companies that simply define themselves by the quality of their customer services. In many industries, especially for firms that sell complicated services or products, superior support and care for customers is a strong competitive advantage.

> Clearly defined goals comprise the measuring stick for every decision you make and every action you take.

Comparing yourself and your product with your competition will help define your position. Sometimes, it is extremely helpful to know what you are not or don't want to do.

What is your objective?

This is the easiest and hardest question. What do you want to achieve? Do you want to launch a specific product/service or your entire company? What is your timeline? Are you aiming for brand recognition or sales numbers? Do you have a revenue goal in mind, or would you be content to break-even? Or, do you just want to enter the market and get your feet wet?

Clearly defined goals form the measuring stick for every decision you make and every action you take. Revisit your objectives frequently. Challenge and question them just as often and do not shy away from adapting your objectives in response to the current situation. Just like in all parts of life, change is the only constant.

How do you want to reach your objective?

With your objective defined, it is time to plan the steps that will allow you to reach it. The extent of your objectives defines how much time and resources you'll need to invest in the effort. It will also function as a guide for the scope of your activities. An objective of, "I just want to get my feet wet," requires different measures than an objective to achieve hard revenue goals.

The more challenging your objective is, the more time you need to invest in planning. The more prepared you are and the more detailed your plan is, the more likely it is you will achieve your goals.

Do you have a plan?

No? Well, as I mentioned, you need one. In fact, you need several plans. First, you need an overall project plan that covers all the details of the entire campaign. This type of plan gives you and your team a work overview, complete with the timeline for when each task will be implemented.

It also describes the relationship between items and how some depend on each other.

Another plan, your communications plan, defines your messages and the channels you'll use. It organizes the outreach part of your activities. An effective communication plan also structures how and in what order you deliver your message to various segments. For example, you could start with a global message and then focus on individual segments.

Then you have your editorial plan. This helps you map out and implement a timeline for when you should publish your message and through what channel. This is the most operational of all the plans you need to create.

Finally, there are more organizational plans such as an escalation plan that helps you keep a cool head and do the right things when you get bad feedback or have adverse events.

I'll remind you again — change is a reality. Although your plan should stand for your best shot at a solid guide, do not write in stone. Do not however, write your plan in the sand, where any little breeze could blow it away. Try to find a good middle ground where you challenge your (solid) plan and even entertain the notion of changing it.

Have you formulated a strategy?

Once you have defined your objective and the steps to get there, you already have some elements of a strategy. The scope of your goals will dictate how time critical it is for you to have a strategy.

Let's look at what it means for you to "have a strategy."

✎ Key take aways

☑ To Do

NYMA

Strategy

Definition of Strategy

Strategy: *A plan of action or policy designed to achieve a major or overall aim.*

"Time to develop a coherent economic strategy."

Synonyms:

Master plan; Grand design; Game plan; Plan (of action); Action plan; Policy; Program

I have heard the word "strategy" overused throughout my professional life. People use it to sound smart or to set a big stage for their idea. I learned some of the things people called "strategies" really were not great grand plans after all. Therefore, I prefer to use evocative synonyms such as "game plan," which expresses very nicely the essence of how you should approach your strategy.

Games are Fun

If you think of a strategy as your game plan, you can answer a few essential questions. The main one is, "What do you want to achieve in a given time frame with the means available to you?" Once you answer this question, it will generate more and new questions about your product, company, target market and audience, mode of product delivery, sales process, and many others. Write those questions down, then think of at least five more questions and answer them as well. The more questions you answer, the more questions you'll uncover. See, isn't that fun? I know, not always, but the exercise is essential.

Sometimes this back and forth is simply the result of deeper thinking on the subject or a response to external feedback. In any case, it is a useful and necessary process.

I've seen this in action in my own life. Every project I have been involved with existed in a state of near-constant up-dating, especially this book. A successful project has the qualities of a living object that changes all the time but can achieve and stick to status-quo. Naturally, there will be times when you must stop, assess, and decide on a plan of attack. You'll need to find the delicate balance between fixed and flux for your project.

Two Ways to Market Your Product

There are two approaches you can take to market your product.

You start with your product and back into the market from there. We call this approach inside-out.

Or, you put your potential target audience at the center and then work back to your product and your company from there. We call this outside-in.

Both are very legitimate ways to think about your game plan. Most of the time you'll use a hybrid. Otherwise, you end up trying to solve the chicken and egg problem. You must work within the context of your individual situation.

If your product is already available and defined, start with the potential target audience. Who would use a product like this and why? Identify the problems it fixes and the needs it caters to. Create a variety of use cases, and then go back to learning as much about your target audience as possible by creating segmentations and personas. You will use these as the basis for every next step.

Sometimes, you haven't defined your service or product yet. In that case, you should look at your product/service first and try to approach it from a new angle. Look for alternative methods and applications for your service/product or, try to extend into new markets. Is your current offering the only way to market your services? Are there secondary capabilities and use cases that you have not considered? Not all uses are straightforward.

Case Study: The Photographer Expansion

A friend asked me how he could expand his business. He is a photographer who wanted to win new customers. We brainstormed, dissected his profession, and got down to the basics of what it meant to be a photographer.

MAIN PROFESSION	Photographer for advertisements and professional portraits
NEW SECONDARY OPPORTUNITIES	Market all the skills required to do the main profession
	Sell photographs he took of landscapes, cities, or moments as pictures online, in galleries, or other retail outlets
	Teach people how to take photographs of their families, friends, landscapes
	Consult on equipment selection and teach clients how to use it
	Enhance pictures taken by other photographers, or teach those skills
	Help agencies/companies plan and organize professional photo shoots

During our brainstorming we uncovered several alternative ways for him to grow his business. He realized he could create more potential in his existing market and create interactive and online solutions to offer his services well beyond his initial reach.

Then, we zoomed out and considered his new potential target audience and the best ways to market to them. This entailed learning as much as possible about their needs and requirements, which happens during the segmentation of the market and customers.

Strategy Models

There are plenty of helpful business tools and models. I like to use the:

- S.W.O.T. Analysis,

- BCG Matrix,

- Porter's Five Forces,

- 4P's of Marketing, or the

- Blue Ocean Method.

You will find the exercises I created for all five of those tools on the NY Marketing Academy website. Take a moment to work through each one because it is important to understand how these models work before you can apply them. With these four models, as well as about 50 other such tools, you can create a clear and easy map that will guide you to the right solution to a problem. Most of them apply to specific scenarios, so look at a few when a strategic question or problem arises.

There aren't many business problems you'll run into that somebody else hasn't experienced and solved. In most cases, you can apply the models developed by consulting firms as safely as a seatbelt in a car. These models are great because they are proven and tested hundreds of times.

Your Objectives Define Your Strategy

Before you start working on your game plan, you must have a clear idea of your goals. The breadth of your objectives defines the scope of your game plan. If you want to make $1,000 per month in a year's time, then your plan requires different urgency than it would if the financial goal is $100,000 per month. Your goals don't have to be financially driven; they could be activity driven, such as produce a certain number of units of your product or see a target number of downloads of your app, or subscribers of your services. Whether driven by your activity, quantities, or market response, your objectives dictate the steps and scope of the actions you take.

When you're defining your goals, it is helpful to break down the numbers, so you have a better understanding of what they mean. For example, if your financial goal is sales revenue of $100,000 per month and your product has a retail price of $10, it means you must sell 10,000 units to reach your goal. This also means you'll need to produce a minimum 10,000 units. Sales numbers like that need multiple outlets, which also means you must overstock those outlets, so you sell as many units as possible. This, in turn, means that you need to produce more than the 10k units discussed, which requires production facilities that can handle numbers like this. Production is just one side of the coin; the other side is distribution and logistics. However, start on the marketing plan even if you have not solved the production and logistic issues yet. Your marketing effort is the keystone if you want to reach average monthly sales of 10,000 units throughout the year.

If you want to reach 100 units/month in the $1,000 example, however, the challenges are much smaller. Fewer units mean less stress on production, marketing, and fewer number of outlets. You still need to do the solid planning and be prepared to face challenges, but more modest objectives drive the game plan and determine what actions you will take.

You also need to consider if the seasons play a factor in your sales numbers. For example, do people still buy your product if it is cold, hot, rainy, or very sunny outside? This is where customer intelligence is relevant again.

In summary, the bigger your goal, the greater the challenges are to achieve that goal and the more detailed and thoughtful your strategy must be.

Example: Different Growth Strategies for Different Goals

So far, we have looked at the various kinds of plans that will help you be as organized as humanly possible. You will find it is a fantastic feeling to have delineated, strategic steps established to best achieve your goals. You will have a greater chance to achieve them if you remember your strategy is decided by those goals or objectives.

Here is an example of how two firms with a similar product but different goals would approach their strategies. Both outfits are stand-alone app publishing companies whose product does not need anything else; they program the app and publish it. The two apps in our example do not require any other online or offline environments. To further clarify, when Uber published its app, it not only needed users but also drivers to provide the service the users would book through the app. Uber had to build a large network of drivers in every market they planned to enter. They also had legal issues around their use of map and navigation services and payment solutions. And yes, there is the tiny matter of their huge legal issues that stem from the market they disrupted.

It is a massive undertaking to create a new ecosystem to support an app like Uber. Therefore, to keep everyone's head from swelling to an unhealthy state, we will exclude firms like that from our example. Instead, we will consider two app publishers with two slightly different objectives.

Publisher one, *Out-of-Garage, Inc.*, wants to achieve a revenue of $1,000 per month when they launch their app. The second publisher, *Make-it-big, Inc.*, has a goal that is slightly more ambitious. They want to sell at least 10,000 units every month, excluding any licenses they give away for free. The price point of both apps is the same: $1.00. Yes, I like to keep it simple.

Scale Dictates Strategy

The individual strategies for each publisher are quite different in scale. It seems easy enough to get $1,000/month in sales on the books, but the essential processes to find even one thousand people who are interested in your app must be in place. You need to have communications and marketing plans that ensure enough lead generation to reach $1,000 in sales every month. Still, 1,000 units/month is manageable, especially if you have a clear idea about who your target audience is and how to approach them. If you are diligent about the plan and simply follow it, you would have a good chance of reaching those kinds of sales goals.

Tenfold that goal and you quickly see added challenges. The lead generation operation of *Make-it-big, Inc.* must reach the same numbers in a month that the *Out-of-Garage, Inc.* guys have a year to achieve. Two guys in a garage may manage to hit those numbers for a month or two, but eventually, their operation will have to be much more professional. As their number of users climbs, they will need a higher level of skills and effort to generate the leads required to attract 1,000 new customers every month. If we apply an average conversion rate of 10% (keeping it simple), that means they must get 10,000 potential customers into their sales funnel — 10,000 new leads every month. At some point, word-of-mouth will generate extra leads they don't have to pursue, but it won't be enough.

The *Make-it-big, Inc.* company, on the other hand, needs to think about dedicated sales agents and lead-generation professionals. Their sales funnel design must be highly professional and convert much more efficiently than that of the folks working out of the garage. A 10% conversion rate may not be good enough, because it means 90% of the people *Make-it-big, Inc.* has motivated to get into their sales funnel, are jumping out. Why is this a problem? Because search engine marketing (SEM), online banners, or similar promotions on social media via Facebook or Twitter costs money every time someone clicks on an ad. If 90% of your traffic creates only costs, it means either you haven't focused your message to only speak to your target audience, or that your lead generation is sabotaged by the sales pages linked from the online ad. With a CPM (cost per mille) of $2.80 for every thousand impressions of your ad and another $0.75 (click-through rate) for every click on your ad, you see how a highly targeted campaign in combination with high conversion rates can make all the difference for your revenue to profit ratio. In our example, *Make-it-big, Inc.* pays $252 to generate 90,000 people who click on an ad worth $67,500, and do not buy anything. With $10,000 in monthly sales, this is certainly not a sustainable business model.

Therefore, *Make-it-big, Inc.* must make sure their non-paid lead generation works at the highest level. Compared to the *Out-of-Garage, Inc.* guys, who can get away with a limited budget for online ad for as long as they are active online, the *Make-it-big, Inc.* sales and marketing team are under much more pressure.

Dealing with customers brings yet another challenge that can surprise people. Users tend to have problems, questions, requests, and they want your attention. In my experience, you will hear from around 2% of your user base if nothing big is going wrong with the product. If you only have a thousand users a month to worry about, that means you are looking at 20 support cases per month. That sounds manageable enough. One of the two guys in the garage can take care of that in 5-minutes a day, if that much. However, the *Make-it-big, Inc.* team are looking at 200 support cases the first month and 2,000 after 10 months. This tenfold thing really comes to a boiling point now. While the garage guys can deal with their 200 support cases 10 months down the road, the *Make-it-big, Inc.* crew now need to think about having a dedicated support person in place.

When we look at the two examples, it is obvious why your objectives drive your strategy. Your marketing, sales, and operational strategies must consider your goals and what impact that will have on your organization's financial resources, people, workplace, equipment, and administrative overhead.

I like to create base, medium, and top cases in which I calculate and describe every scenario so there are no surprises. We don't want the *Out-of-Garage, Inc.* crew to be overwhelmed with an overachieving success that turns them into headless chickens. We also do not want a team of 15 people that only generates $1,000 in revenue with expenses of $100,000.

My top strategy tips:

- Set S.M.A.R.T. goals (See Chapter 8) and create the right strategy to achieve them.

- Write down your goals and include a time for when you want to achieve them.

- Set realistic goals. There is no need to put yourself under pressure to chase after too lofty targets.

Headless
Chicken

- Be ready to overachieve and underachieve.

- Create contingency plans for both noted above.

- Know your target audience and you will save money, therefore, keep reading!

- Wash, rinse, and repeat: Test your campaigns, refine them, and test again on a bigger scale. Then, start over until you reach the scale to achieve your goals.

- Quality, authenticity, and openness are everything to the sustainability of your strategy. Keep reading!

Lastly, strategize growth. Create a strategy to grow your business once you've achieved your goals. An overachievement plan will help you map out what this means for your operational readiness. Growth comes when you apply the intelligence from wash, rinse, and repeat, and what you have learned about your target audience.

> **Growth comes when you apply the intelligence from wash, rinse, and repeat.**

Marketing and Communications

After you have defined your product and services and the scope of your objectives, you then need to describe the more operational elements of the plan. Your communications should evolve from the first engagement of your users to making them returning customers for your products and your brand. The main questions you need to address now include:

- Segmentation: who is your market and your target audience?

- What will your messaging look like?

- Which channels will you use for your marketing communications?

- What is the timeline for each step as you execute the game plan?

- Have you created your project plan as well as a communication plan?

- And finally, for each of the steps before: what tools will you use to achieve your goals?

See Chapter 13 where I illustrate and further describe the customer lifecycle progression from a subscriber or one-time buyer to returning customer.

Time to Get Started!

You will answer those questions in the later chapters. Keep reading and you will find a step-by-step guide, the basic theoretical groundwork, as well as operational tips and tricks for success.

📑 **Topic** **Strategy**

📄 **Workstream**

It is a good idea for all readers to conduct a S.W.O.T. analysis, regardless of your objective or workstream. The S.W.O.T. (Strengths, Weaknesses, Opportunities, and Threats) process examines the internal forces, Strengths and Weaknesses, and external forces, Opportunities and Threats, that influence the success of a product or company.

Find all exercises on www.nycmarketingacademy.com.

A

▶ Review Exercise "4P's of Marketing" and Exercise "Blue Ocean Method," methods that focus on product marketing. Exercise "Porter's Five Forces" is also helpful.

B

▶ Review Exercise "BCG Matrix." Developed by the consulting company Boston Consulting Group, this model examines your entire product line vs. a single product. After you complete the S.W.O.T. analysis, this exercise will help you identify which of your products has the greatest potential. Once you make that decision, please refer to the Exercises in workstream A, but with an emphasis on the brand and company level vs. a product focus.
For additional support, feel free to reach out.

C

▶ Refer to the Exercises referenced for workstreams A and B to learn the most current strategic models.

Answer: What do the models tell you about your campaign, company, or product?

Review and re-evaluate the introduction/executive summary you wrote based on the results of the exercises.

Create a main revenue stream and two alternative ways to create revenue/market a product or services.

✎ Key take aways

☑ To Do

-
-
-
-
-
-
-

Segmentation and Why You Need It

Curiosity is Key, Even in the Military

Segmentation means to divide the marketplace into parts, or segments. But before you can divide the market into segments, you must know your audience.

Segmentation has always been fun for me because I have a general curiosity about people's behavior. Why are they doing what they do? How do they make their decisions? I wonder about simple things, like what they decided to wear that day, why they chose to do a certain thing at that moment, or how they choose the products they use. That is all interesting to me because every detail completes my picture of the people around me and enhances my understanding of them. That innate curiosity sharpened the many relevant marketing skills I use every day.

As I mentioned, this penchant for wondering started long before I got to the PsyOps, and since the German military knows how to conduct a spot-on personnel assessment, they quickly identified my inquisitive nature. Then, when I joined the PsyOps, the German Army gave me tools that allowed me to become even more observant and precise in how I segmented the people around me. It did not take long for my daily mission reports to reflect those sharpened observation skills and precision.

A Little Empathy Goes a Long Way

On my first day or second day in Bosnia in late 1996, we were in a local market in Sarajevo, Bosnia. Even though we looked like turtles in our full gear, helmets, long guns, and radios with 3-foot antennas, we tried to interact with the residents. Every now and then our radios crackled loudly and, without fail, anyone near us jumped back a few feet. It was not easy to talk to people who fear you and your equipment. When I finally managed to talk to someone, I got my first real-life lesson in empathy. He said, "How can you expect us to trust you if you don't trust me. You look like you are ready to engage in a firefight against us while making all those annoying sounds. Sounds that remind us of the war that is barely over." (The Dayton Agreement for Peace was signed in December 2015).

Those words lifted a haze from my eyes. We were so insensitive and self-centered that we had totally forgotten their perspective. The people of Sarajevo were there to buy bread, clean water, and other life essentials, nothing more. For us to gain their trust we had to show that we trusted them, and there was no reason for us to mistrust them. At the time, there were no known reports of aggressive actions against soldiers and it was years before suicide bombings were something people in those situations thought about.

In my report for that day, I covered the conversations I had with the residents and reflected on their message. The very next morning, we received new orders on our dress code. Our superiors told us to leave the heavy armor behind, not to openly wear our weapons, and to look more personable. This changed a lot for us and our dealings with the locals. It also changed everything for me. First, it surprised the socks off me, that a) anyone read those reports, and b) that it would result in immediate reaction and changes. If you have ever worked in the military or any other big organization, you will know, "immediate response" is not what usually happens when a report comes in from a low-level staffer.

Be the General

We learned a lesson that day and marketers should apply it to today's marketing landscape: Go out there and get to know your audience, listen to what they have to say. Digest the information and most importantly, react.

With his speedy response to my report, our commander back then, a General, showed a brisk reaction time that is a must-have in the digital age. When you learn what you are doing is failing, react to it at once.

Unfortunately, or luckily, depending on your angle, your audience will be a bit more diverse than the people in that market in Sarajevo back in 1996. One little thing you learn about your entire audience won't have such a big impact, but if you find a significant detail, make sure you apply that new intelligence immediately. Be the General.

Your audience will be diverse, however, and difficult to grasp. This is where segmentation helps. If you define commonalities to differentiate between two or three groups, you will get a better picture of your audience. Then you can learn about and understand those different market groups.

Disloyal Consumers = Opportunity

> The digital age has empowered consumers like never before; they have choices, and they know how to use them.

The digital age has empowered consumers like never before; they have choices and they know how to use them. In 2021, every company, shop, or service competes with businesses or offers that aren't necessarily from the same neighborhood, city, or even country. Digitalization has transformed business and now firms face global competition. Users know that and play this card to their advantage. Digital trends have made consumers high-maintenance, disloyal, vocal, and well-connected. Although this sounds a bit doom-and-gloomy, it is also an incredible opportunity. Suddenly, you can compete for customers that prior to now were unattainable. The work you do, the more effort you invest to learn about them and to show the value of your product or services to them, the better you will do.

Think of the little sneaker store in Westwood, New Jersey (@sneakerlounge) that reaches a global audience because they use social media and an online store. Now they do not have to move to the expensive store on Bleeker Street in Manhattan's West Village. As a result, they are under less financial pressure.

How can you use segmentation to your benefit? First, make yourself available in the most authentic way possible. Be yourself. Show interest in your customers and learn about who they are. Just like the neighborhood deli owner who knew all the local customers, you must know and understand your target audiences' needs and wants. When you show interest in their feedback, their differences, and overall context, you sharpen your understanding of them. Then you can refine the original segments you created.

Build Customer Loyalty via Relationships

This foundation for a relationship with your customers makes good business sense. Industry research tells us it is much cheaper to keep existing customers and convert them into returning customers than it is to win new customers. A key method to do this is to create beneficial relationships with your customers. Strong customer relationships mean higher customer loyalty, which puts your business at a competitive advantage (Firdaus and Kanyan, 2012). Customer loyalty, and therefore customer relationships, are the building blocks for the sustainability of your business. A loyal customer has less price sensibility because the relationship they have formed with your brand weighs heavily in their decision-making process. The relationship you have formed with them has a monetary value you can use to your benefit.

Successful relationships with your customers also reduce churn. Reduced churn allows sustainable growth in your subscriber numbers. A 10% churn rate and a 30% growth rate at the beginning does not sound troublesome, but we all know the staggering growth rates of the early launch period will fade. After a while, your growth rate will decline and be close to your churn rate. At that point, you are not growing anymore. Now your numbers are stagnant, and you must fight to keep up with your churn rate.

Successful customer relationships can save you from this, and sound segmentation is at the core of such relationships.

The chapter "Customer Success" will talk about how to create sustainable success after your initial launch.

Well-rounded segments and personas will be the keystone for all your efforts.

Segments and Then Personas

Before you create individual personas, you need to complete a high-level segmentation of your customer base. Segment and persona attributes should align with a comprehensive picture of your target market.

Market segments are larger than user personas. Use demographics, geographics, and psychographics to distinguish between segments. Demographics uses age, sex, income, occupation, language, or marital status as distinguishing factors. Geographics uses unique location-based factors such as countries and regions and their characteristics such as climate and other environmental factors, e.g. sea vs. mountain, the Mediterranean vs. Northern lifestyle. Psychographics are behavioral indicators such as opinions, beliefs, or values.

Marketers analyze these three factors to craft an effective strategy to target desired segments. Targeted and efficient messaging guarantees a much higher return on investment (ROI) rates because it specifically addresses the needs, requirements, and expectations of the segment.

The following two definitions will help you better understand the need for segmentation:

- A segmentation basis is a set of variables or characteristics used to assign potential customers to homogeneous groups.

- Segmentation variables are customer characteristics that relate to some crucial difference in customer response to the marketing effort.

Market segments should identify homogeneous groups that differentiate from each other as much as possible. The differences between them will make the resulting segments a success.

A market segment should be:

- measurable,

- accessible by communication and distribution channels,

- different in its response to a marketing mix,

- durable (not change too quickly),

- and large enough to be profitable.

Once you define the general segments, then find even more detailed segmentation, such as:

- Geographic segmentation, based on regional variables such as region, climate, population density, and population growth rate.

- Demographic segmentation, based on variables such as age, gender, ethnicity, education, occupation, income, and family status.

- Psychographic segmentation, based on variables such as values, attitudes, and lifestyle.

- Behavioral segmentation, based on variables such as usage rate and patterns, price sensitivity, brand loyalty, and benefits.

- Customer type, based on factors such as the size of the organization, its industry, position in the value chain, etc.

- Buyer behavior, based on factors such as loyalty to suppliers, usage patterns, and order size.

The next step is the commercial evaluation of each segment.

How big is the opportunity?

What is the expected success rate in the segment?

How good a match is my product for this target audience?

How much must I invest to be successful in this segment?

What is the potential ROI and is it tangible or intangible in nature?

The answers to these questions will help you determine if your segments are valid. If the answers tell you the respective segments are too small, too costly to explore, or have too little potential, you may want to skip those market segments in your go-to-market plan. When you create segments the correct way and invest the time and money to research them, you can trust the results and respond to them.

Get Started with Segmentation

When you segment your market, you break it down into small bits or "segments." First, identify three or more elements like product, company, available structure, and current situation. Then, ask a few essential questions for each element to kick off your segmentation process. Listed below are examples of questions that will get you started. There may be others, but these are a good starting point for your exercise.

The Product

What problem does your product solve?

Try to see the big picture when you answer this question. The details are not as important as determining whether your customers will come from a general audience or a specialized market. Does your product solve a problem that anyone, anywhere in the world could have, or is it only something people who climb mountains higher than 3,000 meters need? Must you position your product so it appeals to a specific target audience, or should you explore different methods to position it for a global audience?

Is your product unique or are there incumbent players already in the market?

This is the easiest and the most research-intense question you will answer. You need to know as much about your competition as possible. Are there players in the market who already offer a solution to the problem your product will solve? If so, how similar are they and where do they play? Will it be easy for you to differentiate within your targeted market, such as by language or by being a local player? Are you/is your quality better or is your product/service easier or more comfortable to use? Although the answers to those questions are more related to product marketing, they may point you toward a specific market direction or a niche.

Although the questions might sound easy, the scrutiny required to get their answers might be the most challenging research so far. The results you undercover could cause you to doubt everything. Do not let it distract you; instead, let this encourage you. Do not be dissuaded from pursuing your dream or your plan just because you discover other companies supply a similar product or service. You should be reassured because there is a market, and that other people or companies have been successful in it. The answers to all the questions in this book will help you find your place in that market. Just stick with the process!

Does your product address a local, regional, national, or global market, and what does that mean?

This should be a simple question to answer and one that will give you an idea the scale to which you must build your operation. This does not necessarily mean you'll hire your first 1,000 employees at once but refers to your choice of language and whether you must consider local/regional restrictions. Once you know the regional scale, you can build use cases for your product based on the different regions. This will help you better understand how your cus-

> You will uncover key factors that help point you toward your segmentation when you figure out who you and your company are.

tomers will use your product. Even though we are not looking at personas yet, you will get an idea of the type of users who could use your product.

You and Your Company

Who are you and who is your company?

When you start your company and assess the opportunities in the market, it makes sense to look at who you are and what sets your company apart. Who are you and what makes you and your company unique, just as good as, or better than anyone else competing in your market? What factors play to your advantage, come easy to you, and which factors will be more of a challenge? Can you solve those challenges with an investment of resources or are they are unsolvable at this point?

You will uncover key factors that help point you toward your segmentation when you figure out who you and your company are.

What Does Your Current Infrastructure Look Like?

Can your current structure support a local operation? How about a global rollout? How much storage room do you have? Are there language or technical barriers and/or strengths that limit or enable you to think global vs. local? Do you have a local store? Do you have resources to build an e-commerce page? Do you have access to global distribution channels or are you reduced to your local post office and their limited hours? Although no single answer will determine your final infrastructure configuration, it may prod you to probe deeper and ask the questions that will lead you to the best solutions for your infrastructural needs.

Why Should a Customer Trust You (More)?

Is trust an important topic when it comes to you and your product? If so, and it often is, how do you make sure you are trustworthy? What quality assurance measures do you have in place to warrant the trust of your customers? Do you have quality processes that distinguish you from your competition and make you better than they are in this regard?

Personas

Personas are archetypical representations of your projected customers or users. Personas, also called buyer personas or archetypes, have a name and a description of their key characteristics such as personal traits, current situation, behaviors, goals, and preferences (Nielsen, L and Storgaard Hansen, K. 2014). well-done personas have a personality with history, needs, and behavioral traits that companies and their various departments use as a foundation for stakeholders. Product development, design, marketing, and communications teams use personas as a key form of guidance that is otherwise not available.

Personas are based on data obtained from surveys, observations, and interviews. Sometimes we build personas based on a combination of the data from those sources and the experience of the person creating the personas.

Building personas can be an arduous process as some stakeholders may not like the emotionless and abstract description of a persona, and others may be uncomfortable with the characteristics and details of a persona. Use different iterations of a persona and customize them to fit the needs of each department.

The Emergence of Personas

One of the challenges any company, especially start-ups, has is limited knowledge about their target audience. Who will use and buy the product? In a perfect world, i.e., perfectly funded, your company would launch a sizable research project that takes months to complete and includes independent data about the market and products like the one you want to launch. With this empirical data about the general market, you would then conduct added product-focused research to get even more specific, and then invite focus groups to discuss the product, marketing, or communication strategies. This is how a traditional marketing department works with other departments like product development and product design or user experience (UX) groups to make sure the product hits the market nerve.

Unfortunately, the business world is just as imperfect as the real world. Usually, you have as little time as you have budget to fund such a research operation. Today's approach also has changed to keep up with the fast-moving markets of the digital age. "Fail fast" is the credo these days, so you need to stay close to your target customers and get immediate feedback instead of months down the road when your perfect product hits the wall.

But still, you need to have an idea for whom you are doing this and what they will think about it. Market feedback is and always will be a must-have.

Living Personas

> Accept change is a constant and that everything you do must be fluid.

Creating buyer personas is a handy method that can enable you to gain an idea about your target audience's situations, their emotions, and requirements to support the next steps of crafting your communication and marketing strategy. Any persona you create based on assumptions, which is a legitimate way to start, will be just as right as it will be wrong. It will, therefore, be important to constantly challenge the personas you have created and to refine them with research and real-life data. Using assumption-based personas will get you started quickly and supplies a dataset against which to compare new data. It is important to regard your personas as living and changing sets of characteristics that will help you getting your marketing operation in place. You also must constantly set out to improve your personas by doing more research.

Let go of the static way of thinking that a persona initially based on your own experience has no real-life application and therefore does not add any value to your processes. Instead, apply a much more agile concept. Accept change is a constant and that everything you do must be fluid. Apply the knowledge you have today, test it tomorrow, and re-apply the new knowledge the day after that. This needs to be a reiterative process. The organization must acknowledge anything that is true today could be dated and false data tomorrow. Trial and error, when executed quickly, is a valid approach to business today because we can collect information much faster and cheaper than ever before. In the digital age, you can reach out to your users and get immediate feedback. You do not have to go out on the streets and search for people anymore. They are all right there – a global audience only a click away. Stay open and take the feedback seriously. Looking for answers and ignoring the ones you got because you did not like them, is not smart and a recipe for failure. Therefore, your digital marketing operation, something we will discuss later in this book, is crucial to your success, especially if you're working with a tight budget. Your digital marketing operation is a bi-directional channel and lifeline to your market and therefore, much more than just a promotional channel.

The Purpose of Personas in Marketing

Personas provide you and your team with a better understanding of your target audience. Personas will help you visualize the intelligence you gathered about your market. Well-created personas should have hard-cut descriptions that you have clearly differentiated. They will serve as building blocks of intelligence when you create messaging, packaging, pricing, for research and defining your communication channels, and much more. As I have mentioned multiple times in this book already, your marketing must be customer centered. You can only be successful with that if you have a good understanding of who your users and sub-segments are. Well-crafted and researched personas will provide that knowledge.

The personas that you build – the Toms, Johns, and Marys – need to be detailed enough to answer several questions: Who is your target audience and what does their journey from need to research to interest to purchase look like? Your personas should tell you about the traits your customers share and those that make them different. All are crucial data points you must consider in your messaging.

The more detail you have, the better. On the flip side, you should not be too granular with your personas as that will make them too specific and they will represent too small a sample size of your audience. Finding the right balance is important.

Personas help you learn about your customers' research behavior and the external factors that might influence their decision-making process. Your created personas should tell you what Tom needs to know to buy your product and why John will not react to the same message that Mary does. Find the common denominator; this will help you create a universally powerful sales message that reaches as many of your personas as possible.

Well-designed personas help you create effective communication that engages and guides your potential customers along the path to a successful transaction.

How to Create Personas

You will not create powerful user or buyer personas overnight. Think of personas as living organisms that must grow as long as your product line or company exists. The more developed personas are, the more will they help you better understand your target audience.

So, the first step in creating good personas is a healthy guessing game. Based on your general segmentation, build out smaller groups or individuals by narrowing down factors of demographics, psychographics, or geographics. An effective way to do this is start with one factor that is most important for success, i.e. consumer vs. business user. Once you identify this, it will lead to more factors that could be crucial. One factor like this can determine the size, type, or industry of a business target or demographics for a consumer. After you find these denominating factors, then you can build out differences which will create actual personas.

Distinctions are the Name of the Game

Next, find distinguishing factors that put the user persona at the center. What is the perceived or desired use of the product? What value or benefit will the respective persona gain with the product? It is crucial to match the different behavior patterns of the persona groups to better evaluate the commercial value of each persona. At this point, you must carefully monitor the number of commonalities as well as differences between the personas. A high number of personas can be counterproductive at the beginning. Focus on describing specific traits that distinguish one persona from the other. These distinctions help you create differentiated messaging for each.

The best approach is to start very broadly and create a maximum of two or three personas. The more experienced and granular you become, the more personas you will develop. Just be careful not to overdo it. It is not necessary or cost-effective to find the three guys on an island who might use your product once every full moon. Your objective is to reach all of Manhattan, the Americas, Europe, or the world, and make yours a global product. In short, your goal is to scale your business and find customer groups that will help you generate maximum revenue at highest efficiency. Although those three guys on the island might become your hardcore fans, they are not the scale on which you should build your business.

Next, set a thesis about who your personas are from your point of view. Then, as with any good thesis, you must test it. Not once, but repeatedly. Do the research, apply what you have learned, and test it again. That way, you will develop true customer insights based on hard and dependable intelligence.

It is a process, so put in the work.

I. Five Categories used to Create Personas

BUSINESS	CONSUMER
BACKGROUND	
Job Title	Age
Age	Gender
Education	Family Status
Income	Education Level
Years in Role	Language
	Location
	Excluding Location
SITUATION	
Priorities	Career Level
Pain Points	Job Title
Motivation	Financial Status
Needs	Health
Objectives	Accomondation
PERSONAL	
Interests	Interests
Mentality	Mentality
Behaviour	Behaviour
Ambitions	Ambitions
Fears	Fears
Rival	
HABITS	
Likes & Dislikes	Likes & Dislikes
Habits	Habits
Skills	Skills
Media Consumption	Media Consumption
Research Methods	Buying Preparations
Trusted Resources	
DECISIONS	
Reporting Lines	Purchase Process
Buying Power	Information Resources
Budget	Decision Resources
Key Stakeholder	
Purchasing Process	

II. Example for a Persona Card

CATEGORY:
Business or Consumer

PICTURE:

SITUATION:

HABITS:

PERSONAL:

BACKGROUND:

DECISION

More Thoughts on Personas

One person can have multiple personas based on behavior or context.

We will call these "situational personas," and you will know what this means once you think about it. For example, the decisions I make differ quite a lot if I make them like a father, husband, or in the context of my work when it comes to travel, for example. I rent different cars when I travel alone or for business than I do if I go with my wife or with the entire family. Does that make me a different person? No. But it changes what I need and require based on the context of my situation. Staying with the travel example, you can continue and work out the differences on which hotels I choose, how I organize my meals, or how I spent my time at my destination.

For work related travel, I am very task focused. I concentrate on getting there and getting ready for the meetings or events I am attend. The less noise or disruption I have between me and my objective, the better it is. In that context, I value efficiency the most. Whatever product or service helps me increase this efficiency will interest me and catch my attention – ideally before I leave or in such a way that I can get back to it later. Just do not take my time away.

When traveling with my family, efficiency is only secondary. Experiencing time with my family is my primary objective. Comfort for all and entertainment for my son is paramount. The quality of the time I spend is more important than being efficient, quick, or productive. I create, modify, or completely change plans on the fly.

However, none of it makes me a different person, just a different person or persona in the respective situations.

People evolve from one persona to another.

Just as I change my situational behavior based on the context in which I move at the time of my travels, I also change and evolve in a different timeframe. From soldier to someone working and owning an agency. From being single or dating to being married with children. From living alone in a small apartment in Germany to living in a house in the New York metropolitan area. My demographics, socio-ecological conditions, and overall interests have changed. Allow for these changes to happen and be ready to move individuals within your audience from one persona to another. A good reason to stay in touch with your audience is so you can understand those changes. All the data points you collect about your customers are relevant because they allow you to verify their affiliation with one persona or another.

Personas change during the customer lifecycle.

A few years ago, I researched and finally bought a license for some research software for my Open-Xchange work. At this point, I did not have a perfect understanding of what I would need or how it all worked in-depth. In the past, I outsourced research, but now I wanted to get a better understanding of how it works and to stay closer to the process of generating surveys and reports. The topics I needed to research were too important to not fully be in control of the process from a to z.

I had to learn how the software worked and what the market was like for research software. I learned more about tricks and best practices, as well as which features were more important than others. This new knowledge resulted in me canceling the first software and moving on to another provider that was better able to cater to our needs and to work at a scale that made sense for us. These surveys would get response numbers in the thousands, if not even more. With that comes a vast amount of data that you need to analyze quickly, preferably with a great deal of automation and support of AI. If you have open text answers, you want to be able to have a powerful sentiment analyzes built-in because you do not have the time nor the resources to read all responses promptly. Specific keywords, like good, bad, liked, disliked, hated, loved, to list a few, are critical indicators to what a person means. Mix that with key product names or features, and you quickly get an idea of what comments appear in which context and whether they are positive or negative in their sentiment.

All this I learned. From being a basic user when I bought the first software license, I became a customer unhappy with this vendor and a more demanding one with a much different understanding of the product for the next group of vendors I considered.

My skill level changed or evolved, and with it, my persona did as well. I was no longer the unsure new user, but a customer who wanted software that could at least fulfill my enterprise if not corporate needs, based on the Fortune 500 customers I work with around the globe.

Do not forget about Negative Personas.

When you're creating personas, you may also create negative personas, almost by accident. Those are just as valuable as the positive personas are because they allow you to exclude groups of people who are not your target audience when it is time to look at campaigns, communications, or promotions. Knowing who is not part of your audience is a useful data point to have.

A

▶ Answer: What market segments do your competitors target?

▶ Answer: How does your competitors' target audience differ from yours and why?

▶ Create market segments based on the differences between your target audience and your competitors'. If they sell to small businesses and you sell to residential customers, what additional factors are different about your respective buyers?
How are the two markets similar?

▶ Create personas based on the market segments you created.
Use "Five categories to create personas" and "Example for a Persona Card" as guidance.

▶ Identify how you can differentiate your company/brand from that of your competitors. How are you different than your competitors? How does this differentiation impact your target audience? Create market segments based on how they differ from your competitors.

▶ Create personas based on the market segments you created. Use "Five categories to create personas" and "Example for a Persona Card" as guidance.

▶ Apply the steps in workstream B to your brand/company.
Are these segments defined for your company? If so, review and
test the definitions.
Identify and define additional market segments.

▶ Create personas based on the market segments you created.
Use "Five categories to create personas" and "Example for a Persona
Card" as guidance.

✏️ Key take aways

☑️ To Do

NYMA

Marketing and Communication Strategy

At this point, you have crafted your strategy, defined your market segments, and started to build personas so you can better understand the distinct groups within your target audience.

Now you need a defined plan that outlines your marketing and communication strategy. Everything you have done so far was preparation for these next steps.

> Today, every customer wants you to build a relationship with her at her pleasure, but she can decide to leave anytime she wants.

New Technology = New Marketing Tools

Marketing and marketing communication have changed drastically over the past few decades, and most dramatically so in the last ten years. The emergence of the internet, email, and web 2.0 changed how we approach marketing and communication today. Marketers now have shiny new tools in their arsenal they could have only dreamt of in the 1980s. At the same time, their target audience is more complicated than ever before. The days are over when the only things a marketer had to think about were booking TV promotions, news ads, or a billboard placement. At that time, the only relationships marketers had to build were with the gatekeepers in the press or the people who controlled retail placement.

Today, every customer wants you to build a relationship with her at her pleasure, but she can decide to leave anytime she wants. Even worse, your competition will make it as easy as possible for her to switch loyalty. They are happy about all the work you did to segment her and promote the level of service she now expects. Now your competition is in the position to make a better offer to win her over.

Although this is a little simplified, it is the essence of the brave new world of marketing in the 21st century.

It is important to remember that marketing today involves your entire organization. If a problematic situation arises with a customer during a sales, support, or any interaction with your company, that customer can now reach a lot more people than her friends at the hair salon or simply complain to her neighbors about it. She may tell your entire target audience how she felt mistreated or that your product did not live up to your promises. If you are lucky, she simply got a better offer from your competitor next door and quietly slipped away. That old cliché that everyone in a company is in sales is truer than ever. Any one of your employees' external encounters can lead to a public relations nightmare.

For this reason, among others, your company needs a holistic and fully integrated approach to marketing and marketing communication. Each member of your company must know and buy into your marketing and communication strategy. The success of your company depends on it.

Integrated Marketing: A Holistic Approach to Marketing and Communication

"Integrated marketing" sounds easy enough to understand. All marketing should be coordinated and orchestrated, so all efforts are synchronized, right? Not so fast, it is not as easy as it sounds.

Integrated marketing touches all aspects of organizational life. The entire organization must buy into all the company's goals and understand its vision and mission statements.

This effort starts with the company's leadership and reaches throughout the ranks to the intern. Everyone must understand why the company does what it does and what makes it great, unique, and a trustworthy partner for any customer. In the organizational context, this means human resources, internal administration, and all other departments are in the loop and get clear guidelines for communication with external audiences. Even staff who are less in touch with the lofty long-term strategies of a company must understand and internalize the firm's communication protocols and goals. Organizations whose employees are involved in the process to achieve a greater good, the success of the firm, enjoy improved internal communication and increased motivation, the heart and soul of a strong company.

> The primary purpose of your communication efforts must be to positively influence the attitude of your customers.

Although internal communication and how to ensure cooperation and company-wide spirit would be an interesting topic to dive into, it is deep enough to write an entirely different book on the subject. Therefore, we will zoom out and focus solely on external communication intended for marketing and sales.

For all customer-focused marketing and communication efforts, you must consider some basic yet crucial elements. As you can see in graphic III, "Integrated Marketing Communication," all marketing channels be must integrated — inbound or outbound channels, interactive or passive properties your customers touch knowingly or not — everything must be in sync.

Basic and Generally Agreed-Upon Rules of Marketing

Most marketing communication scholars and practitioners prescribe the following guidance:

1. The primary purpose of your communication efforts must be to positively influence the attitude of your customers. Therefore, all communication centers around its effect on customer behavior.

2. To have this positive impact on the customer's attitude toward your product and company, the customer must stand at the center of all communication. This starts when you craft the communication strategy and design the marketing message. It is much more effective to start with the customer and then back into a strategy rather than to start internally, develop a message, and then work toward the customer. If you start internally you risk missing intelligence about what your customer needs.

3. Remember your target audience, your customers, are your partners or potential partners with whom you want to build a long-term relationship. These relationships, just like the ones you have in your private life, should be nourished and treated with care and respect; they require constant effort. The moment you take the relationships you established with your audience for granted, is the moment when you start to lose them. It is extremely difficult to get estranged customers back, and even more expensive.

4. As part of your integrated marketing strategy, you should harmonize all communication efforts and channels and use them authentic to their purpose. Your message must be consistent across all the

channels you use. Any deviation will confuse and lead your audience to doubt if your brand is authentic.

5. Although roles and responsibilities may differ, all communication on the promotional and campaign level must align with general corporate messaging.

6. There must be a single point of coordination for all outgoing communication.

III. Integrated Marketing Communication

How to Create a Marketing Communication Strategy

The purpose of any marketing strategy is to move your target audience through a series of steps during which they evolve from learning about you, your company, or your product to a point where they repeatedly buy your products and suggest them to their social circle.

To achieve this, your communication strategy must be rooted in your company's strategy. What are the goals of the marketing communication? Are those objectives aligned with your target audience's needs? If so, then match your company's communication matrix (Table IV: Messaging and Communication Matrix) with the objective to, "transform a potential customer into a repeat customer."

Use the communication matrix as guidance to create a communication strategy and basic messaging plan, the backbone of your overall communications. Consult the matrix when you launch a new product or when a year or so has passed between promotions. Are the answers you put into your matrix 12 months ago still true and correct today? Revisit and challenge each of the answers and messages you originally compiled to confirm your approach has your customer of today in focus, not your customer of a year ago. Your target audience could be a fast-moving one and often change their habits. The younger your audience, the more often you must update your communication matrix to keep pace with their tempo.

IV. Messaging and Communication Matrix

Messaging Objectives	What do you want your positioning and messaging to accomplish?
Messaging Strategy	How will you achieve the objectives?
Category	What market category do you occupy?
Vision	What is your aspirational market vision (e.g. bottle of your wine on every table)?
Mission	What is your company mission vis-à-vis the vision (e.g. to be the largest producer of good wine)?
Need / Problem	What is the market, business, or user needs you will address?
Position Statement	What is the core positioning statement for the business?
Value Proposition	What is the core value proposition for the business or product?
Key Messages	Craft the key messages you want to consistently convey.
Company Description	Concisely convey who the company is. Create 100, 50, and 25-word versions of this.
Product Description	Concisely convey what the product does. Create 100, 50, and 25-word versions of this.
How it works	Concisely convey how the product or technology works.
Elevator Pitch	Craft your elevator pitch: · Statement to garner attention · Sentence on needs addressed · Sentence on the benefit of your approach · Sentence on how this is different than the competition · Closing call to action

Create Content

All the work you have done up to this point has prepared you for this moment. It is time to create content and identify the messaging format you will use to communicate with your target audience.

Once you gather genuine intelligence about your customers and define your communication strategy, it is all about creating the content and the messaging pieces you will use during the entire communication cycle. All the information you have gathered will serve as the foundation for the content you will now create for the duration of the campaign.

There are many ways to create this core content. Once again, the target audience is at the center of what you want to say. There are a few different basic kinds of copy you will create as part of your messaging plan. You will then use this content across the different communication channels. The core pieces of copy you will need are:

- *Key Selling Proposition* (KSP) – a list of key arguments and benefits crafted specifically to speak to your target audience or a subset, such as a segment or a persona. The KSPs are the first list of benefits and sales-drivers you will create.

- *Value Proposition* – concise text that defines benefits to your target audience in the predefined form of a value proposition. You will find the exercise of creating the value propositions extremely helpful, but also time-consuming. Do not try to complete it 100% in one sitting, but see it as a living and evolving document that you work on continuously.

- ***25, 50, 100 Word Descriptions*** – quick descriptions of predefined length, ready to use in different outlet. You will need these summaries for the press, events, profiles on social media, and many other situations. These ready-to-use copy containers will make your communications game an efficient well-oiled machine.

Value Proposition

When we research value proposition in scholastic papers and journals, we quickly see a well-considered and thoughtful value proposition is "the essence of strategy" and a crucial cornerstone of any company's marketing and communication strategy. We formulate a value proposition because we want to clearly articulate the value of our product, service, or solution. Value is intangible and subjective to the person who is evaluating the good or service we put before him. Because of this, we emphasize the value of the product or service to the potential customer. While a consumer's perspective might be, "how does this help me," a business customer will also calculate the return on investment (ROI).

So, a value with a singular proposition must fulfill two main objectives:

- Speak to the audience

- Describe the value of your product to that audience

Anyone who reads your value proposition should quickly understand:

- What the product is about and how it solves problems or enables the reader to do something new (relevancy)

- The value and benefits the product provides (quantified value)

- Why a consumer should buy the product from you rather than from the competition (unique differentiation)

An effective value proposition, therefore, does not confuse the reader with complicated formulations or too much jargon.

When we define what a value proposition is, we must also look at what it is not. It is not an advertising claim. The carmaker Audi, for example, would not include their claim, "Vorsprung durch Technik / leading through technology," in a value proposition. A value proposition also does not position the product or service in the market environment.

Key take aways

To Do

-
-
-
-
-
-
-

NYMA

Messaging

After you create the value propositions, it is time to translate them into marketing messages for public relations, advertising, or social media communications.

Adjust the messaging for each channel, based on the value proposition and the targeted user.

The message must follow the basic rules of the value proposition but have more of a marketing drive. The messaging must:

- Introduce the product, the market, and the target users

- State clearly what needs and pain points the product addresses

- Describe how it solves those problems

- Present references that prove past performance

- Show why and in what areas the presented product is superior to the competition and solves the problem better

The messaging should tell the truth and present it in a believable way. Lying and misrepresentation have legal ramifications and hurt the product or company's reputation in the market.

Content Marketing Best Practices

As with so many other topics, there are a multitude of things you can and should do, and even more ways to approach the subject of content marketing. However, there are some clear must-dos that you will find on any list and in any article or book on content marketing, such as:

- Offer your audience value with quality content.

- Tie the content to your product, company, and market, without making it one blatant sales pitch after the other.

- Create engaging and user-involved content.

- Obey local rules and regulations, especially if there is the slightest chance of reaching the European market. You need to be aware of the GDPR implications and what you can and cannot do. Your enthusiastic efforts to expand your audience via email may have a costly outcome.

Although these are nice points and certainly correct, they are too general to use as a sustainable guideline for your content marketing efforts. Therefore, I created the list below to give you a more granular and detailed approach with precise directions.

Users First

As I have emphasized throughout this book, everything you do should be centered around the effort that highlights you, your company, brand, product, and team to your audience. Well-utilized marketing content is the first point of contact and business card your audience sees from you. As such, support your audience with content as much as possible.

User Needs and Problems

Because you will be so knowledgeable about your target audience, you can communicate how your product or service will solve users' problems and cater to their needs instead of just hitting a certain number of keywords in your text. Do not get me wrong, keywords are important, but value offers to your audience always comes first.

The experience your audience has with your content is more important than your SEO or SEM efforts. User-shared content and positive comments have a higher impact on brand value than anything else, and if your content is good, users will share it and make positive comments. An engaging blog post or a spot-on tweet that leverages the network and goes viral has far more promotional value than the actual cost to produce the content.

Solicit Feedback from your Users

Do not be afraid to get feedback from your audience. Interaction and a mind open to feedback adds considerable value for you and builds trust with your audience. In my decades of customer interactions, I have learned customers appreciate when I ask for their feedback because it shows I value their opinion. Take it one step further. Do not just respond to them, seek their feedback after you have fixed an issue or improved something they critiqued or already liked. Content marketing is about engaging your audience and there is nothing better than asking your audience for help.

By the User, for the User

User-generated content (UGC) is the crown jewel of content marketing. There is absolutely nothing that has a more positive impact on your efforts than when users create content for you and share their experiences. This gives you testimonials about the quality of your product or services that you could not make about yourself without the appearance of a hard sell. Just remember to reward the users who invest their time, creativity, and/or money to create content for you. You don't need to send them a check, but you should honor them openly and share their work.

Build a Brand, Not Keyword-Friendly Content

Not everything is about SEO. I get it, algorithms, automation, and data science are part of marketing today and, indeed, are especially important. I won't dispute it. In fact, I often promote that approach because it makes marketing processes more transparent and based on predictable behavior.

> **Do not forget that your audience is real, live human beings.**

The text on your website, your blog or in your emails, however, can be too scientifically generated. Do not forget that your audience is real, live human beings. Therefore, when you write copy, you should keep the needs for your audience in mind first and subordinate your SEO needs to that primary objective.

Deliver Value at Every Interaction (Without Talking about Yourself)

Your well-connected audience is an unforgiving audience, and even spoiled. For example, I admit it, if the most recent edition of a newsletter I subscribe to offers me nothing of interest, I unsubscribe. My patience for inbound messaging is at an all-time low and getting worse. This is exacerbated because there are thousands of other sources for information that are just as good or offer more value to me at that point. Be careful what content you put in front of your audience.

Create Content Specifically for Your Target Audience

One-size-fits-all is a concept that rarely works anywhere and is even less effective for content marketing. Your clients are not all the same. They have unique needs and expectations. Your homework with customer segmentation and feedback-based content will help you put the right message in front of your audience.

Enrich digital content with buttons and links based on keywords. And, as we all learned from Amazon, you can channel users to more personalized (segmented) content when you inform them, "Customers who read this also like. . ." I have had enormous success using this self-segmentation tactic. Feedback buttons and subscription lists also allow you to narrow down proffered content choices.

> **One-size-fits-all is a concept that rarely works anywhere and is even less effective for content marketing.**

Personalize Content for Users

The goal of focused content is to deliver a personalized message, specific to each customer. Smart automation and thorough segmentation will help you with that. The more detailed and customized the content is, the better it will work. For example, any message that addresses me by my name gets a different level of attention than an anonymous message. If you have the information, use it, and send Tom Johnson or Jessica Smith their own content. Keep in mind, content delivered with relevant context for Tom or Jessica will get even more of their time and attention.

Sell Subtly

Everyone understands you want to sell a product or service. Since this is a given, you do not need 'buy here' buttons everywhere. It is not necessary or good practice to mention your product and brand in every fifth sentence. You are well positioned if your audience spends time in your eco system. Every sell should be subtle or occur naturally within the flow of how the user digests your content.

It is most important to create brand recognition, loyalty, and return visits to your ecosystem. Do not try to hide the fact that you are trying to sell a product or service. Be clear and deliver a sales message that adds value to your audience.

This is the fine line to walk, but it is well work it.

Focus on Conversions

When it is time to sell, do precisely that. Do it openly and make it easy for your audience. Do not hide the call-to-action; tell your audience what you want them to do next. Make sure your users quickly grasp the value your product/service offers and make it easy to pull the trigger and buy it. When prospects in the sales funnel get distracted or have time to rethink their purchase, conversion rates take a hit. Now is a good time to reference Steve Krug's book, "Don't make me think!" As Krug recommends, make sure the path to buy your product is clear and fast. To quote a friend who helped me while I worked on this book, they can always cancel the order and the account, right? Please do not be hesitant to sell; your business depends on it.

Wash, Rinse, and Repeat

Many marketing experts and practitioners have different opinions about the best time in the process to unveil new content. Some people wait until everything is perfect before they launch, and then there are those who can react quickly to a given market situation and change course on a dime. I like the approach of "failing fast," which at its core is an iterative process that constantly seeks to improve.

For example, when I launch a website with my customers, we create a version zero and get it in front of our audience quickly so we can get their feedback. We then use their reactions to improve the website before we test it again with a wider audience. There are many active and passive ways to collect data about the performance of a website. Social media, open rates, and more, supply a wide range of intelligence which allows you to constantly change your content and measure its reception and conversion rates.

The iterative process will keep your content fresh and ensure constantly improving quality.

Content Marketing Terms every digital marketer needs to know

- **On Demand**

Content or information that is available whenever users want to access it.

- **Inbound/outbound marketing**

Content or information your users have access to when they want to versus content that you send them.

- **Social Channels**

All social media channels such as platforms like Twitter, Instagram, Google, Twitter, Facebook, Pinterest, Snap Chat, Yelp, Meetup, or others

- **Influencer Marketing**

Marketing efforts that focus on reaching key people for a segment. Influencers can be general stars whom everyone knows. More likely, however, they have a significant reputation, following, and ubiquitous presence on social networks.

- **Push vs. Pull communication/advertisement**

An advertiser, like a brand, company, or manufacturer, actively "pushes" information to the customer. But in "pull" communications, the customer actively pursues information about the desired topic, product, or service

- **Owned, earned, or paid exposure/media**

Owned media are websites, blogs, or social channels owned by the company or business owner. Earned media is content produced by users or media outlets that engage, share, or actively contribute. Paid media is promotional messages you pay for, placed in the feeds of users of a channel, or paid articles in the news or specialized media.

- **Webinars**

Webinars are video- and web-based presentations. They are usually live events the user must join at a scheduled time. The best practice, however, is to offer both the live online seminar and a recording of the live event that users can access on demand.

- **Blog, Vlog, podcasts**

Blogs are websites that publish content about specific, often specialized content. However, many popular blogs are hosted by individuals who write about their travels, cooking, healthy living, beauty, or any other topic. Vlogs are the video form of blogs in which people record on video the information about their chosen topic, and post those as videos on channels like YouTube or their website.

- **Podcasts**

Much like Blogs and Vlogs, podcasts are regular publications, but the format is audio. The most successful podcasts are recordings of radio or TV shows, or the podcast host presents aggregated content. Podcasts can also feature interviews with the host and guests to their podcasts.

- **White papers**

These are in-depth reports often used in IT or highly specialized and complex environments to discuss and introduce new concepts, products, or services. In an IT environment, the PR team supplies white papers to industry analysts and other opinion leaders to announce a new service and gain media attention.

- **Social buzz, viral/mouth-to-mouth**

When a topic generates a lot of interaction on social media channels, and people engage at a high clip.

- **Trending topic**

A trending topic has generated buzz around the country, or even across the globe, and Twitter, Instagram, and comparable channels list it as a trending topic.

- **Search Engine Optimization (SEO)**

Although you should optimize content for all browsers, there is no question that we could call Search Engine Optimization, "Google Search optimization." The rules and algorithms that rank your content change often. The more optimized with the right keywords or topics a website, blog, or video channel is, the better its ranking.

- **Search Engine Marketing (SEM)**

In Search Engine Marketing, when someone searches on Google, Bing, or Yahoo! for a topic or keyword, paid advertisements related to that topic appear.

- **Backlinks**

Backlinks are links on other webpages that point to the owned website or blog. The number of backlinks is another important criterion for SEO ranking.

- **Public Relations (PR)**

Public relations are all efforts a company undertakes to communicate with the public. In general, PR used to focus more on traditional media. However, social media channels have become essential, so now, all PR agencies offer them in their portfolio.

Chapter

📖 **Topic** Create Content

📝 **Workstream**

A B C

You'll create a marketing tool box once you complete the messaging and communication matrix in Chapter 10.3.

Create each item listed in this chapter with a special focus on the following points:

- Create content based on what you defined in the messaging matrix.
- Create content that is informative, helpful, and truthful.
- Create valuable content targeted specifically to your market segment.
- Decide if your market segments have changed, and if so, go back to the exercise and apply the changes.
- Or decide if you miscalculated a market segment, and if so, refine your content.

✏️ **Key take aways**

☑️ **To Do**

Public Relations

Public Relations (PR) departments have overseen the public face of companies for the past 100 years. They held relationships with important stakeholders firmly in their hands, decided what was communicated to the public and determined the company's position on all matters. Public relations professionals still serve this very role in many companies today, and rightfully so. However, the emergence of social media has changed this quite

> **Although PR still needs to have a seat at the table when we discuss messaging and external communication, it is no longer the only player.**

a bit, which is why we talk about communication channels and not just PR. Although PR still needs to have a seat at the table when we discuss messaging and external communication, it is no longer the only player. There are faster and more direct feedback channels that cost less and have a bigger and quicker impact. This is especially true if you are not a big corporation that garners massive attention from all the major news outlets who then distribute your story via every available channel, including online.

Nothing changes when we talk about the quality of the message. Content still needs to be interesting and customized for the target audience to create any kind of reaction. The difference is, there are no gatekeepers. The New York Times, et al., no longer exclusively decide whether a topic is newsworthy. Decades ago, they could make or break a story. Now, news breaks to all of us, often at the same time. Social media channels have changed the game for PR. Now, often, the traditional news reports do not create the buzz in the social sphere. Whether it is a U.S. president who tweets from his personal Twitter account or sports megastars who communicate via Instagram when they have decided to change teams, we are all as tuned-in as we are connected directly to the source. No gatekeepers necessary.

What does this mean for PR? Is there still a place for a PR manager in a company, or should we just hire a group of 20-year-olds to handle the digital arena?

The Reports of PR's Death are Greatly Exaggerated

Public Relations and its outlets have adapted to the digital age and are here to stay. Online articles spread like wildfire on the very day of their release and spark conversations in the digital sphere, mostly in social media. This is where PR can and should play a leading role in the communication mix.

The PR manager of today is still the main content creator. She owns the "voice" of a company and manages key relationships with important stakeholders such as analysts, industry press, blogs, or specific individuals. The PR manager works in concert with the digital department, which owns the instant outlets that give the PR manager of today more power than she ever had during the "gatekeeper" years.

Use traditional PR for big announcements, thought leadership, or reputation or crisis management. The language for the PR channel is usually formal and follows the general rules of press release publishing. Although you can handle PR in-house, I suggest you find a PR agency or freelancer who has the necessary contacts to the best traditional, or nondigital, outlets. There are still people who read magazines, even if they read them digitally on their tablets.

If you own a business in the tech and digital industry, you must court key players and turn them into multipliers, or influencers, for the cause. You can buy influence by entering into a contract with the key players for PR, i.e., public awareness and support. Analysts and researchers are part of this group. Although it will be clear these articles were "paid for," this tactic allows you to use their relationships, reach, and connections. If your product lacks quality though, the analysts' reviews will reflect that as they must consider their reputations.

V. The Key Elements of PR

- Press Releases
- Press Relations
- Analyst Relations
- Crises & Change Communication
- Article Placements
  - Proactive
  - Paid
- Tracking Editorial Calendar

Industry peers who are champions of your product and company, or even partners, are also important. Joint press releases or a guest blog on their outlets will lend you and your product more credibility. Of course, as with all other channels or forms of public relations, this is a give and take and all about the value the relationship brings to both sides.

The best way to spread news fast to a big audience is with press releases. This only work when the story you want to spread is newsworthy, and you send it to the right distribution list. Make sure your PR team has access to the important gatekeepers in your industry and they will read what you send them. If that is not the case, then you must use an external agency to make those connections and establish a reputation for you or, simply be consistent with your work and grow your network organically. As is the case with any organic growth, however, it does not happen overnight.

Solid work, bought editorials, and relationship management will establish you in the right circles. But, since you will spend money either way, you may want to save time and work with an agency or a good freelancer right from the start.

Create a Successful Story

There are five basic storylines that draw people in like a bee to nectar. If you combine a couple of those compelling narratives in one article, you have a good chance of creating a winning story.

1. **Underdog good vs. overpowering evil** – We all love stories in which the unlikely hero fights against evil. It is a classic. We all root for the for the hero of the story, unless you are Barney Stinson, the legendary character of the TV show "How I met your mother," who cheered on Johnny Lawrence's character instead of Daniel, the Karate Kid, played by Ralph Macchio.

2. **Scandalous and oddity** – Yes, admit it, you read these stories too. No further explanation needed.

3. **Conflict, suspense, or emotion** – Any of these three automatically pulls us in. We all like the emotional roller coaster we get from a good story. It does not have to be a love story; it could be a story about conflict and dislike. Just look at how well ar-

ticles do that cater to one side of the political aisle while bashing the other.

4. **Celebrities** – Kardashians. Need I say more?

5. **Stick with what's popular** – If everything else fails, just stick with what others are writing about. What worked for their story has potential to work for you as well, if you are close enough to the story (immediacy, proximity).

Communication Channels

Communication channels have their own rules and should play their own roles. I suggest you define those roles before you adopt the messaging.

VI. Example of Content Use Across Different Channels

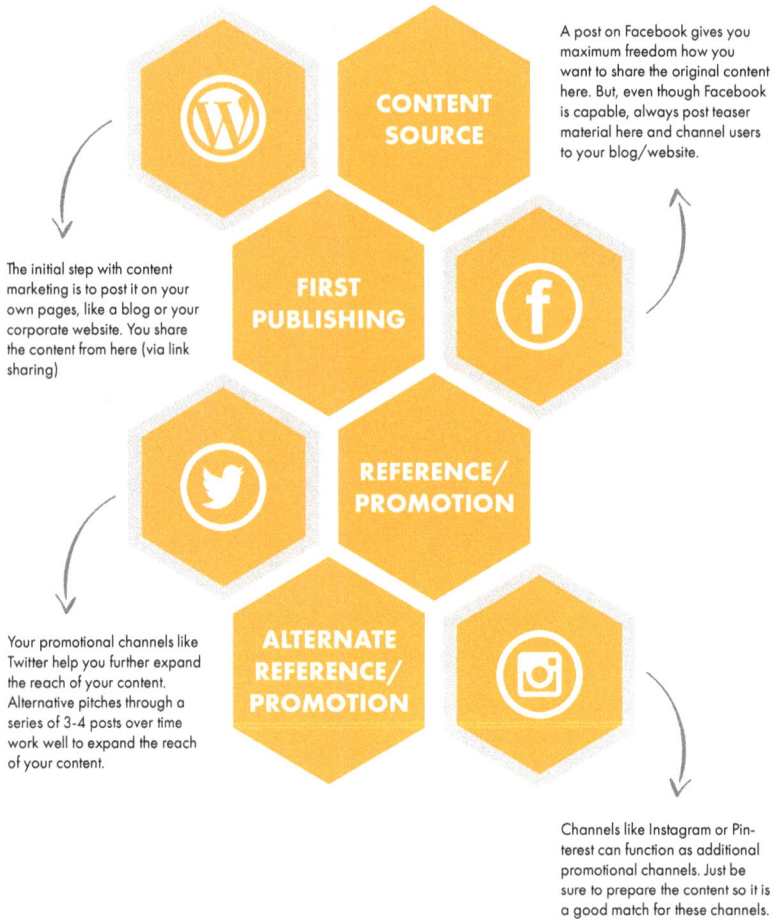

A post on Facebook gives you maximum freedom how you want to share the original content here. But, even though Facebook is capable, always post teaser material here and channel users to your blog/website.

CONTENT SOURCE

The initial step with content marketing is to post it on your own pages, like a blog or your corporate website. You share the content from here (via link sharing)

FIRST PUBLISHING

REFERENCE/ PROMOTION

Your promotional channels like Twitter help you further expand the reach of your content. Alternative pitches through a series of 3-4 posts over time work well to expand the reach of your content.

ALTERNATE REFERENCE/ PROMOTION

Channels like Instagram or Pinterest can function as additional promotional channels. Just be sure to prepare the content so it is a good match for these channels.

VII. Example for Digital Marketing Channels and Roles

	Role	Listen	React	Engage	Communication	Entertainment
Messaging Objectives	Main Content Source Target for channeling	No	No	No	Push directly, pull via directing towards other Channels + Email/Phone/ Forum	Specific campaign sub-sites
Company Blog	Content Source Target for channeling	No	Yes Market News	Yes Thought Leadership content	Passively Interactive (Like, Share, react w/ other channels)	No
Leading communication driver (e.g. Twitter, LinkedIn)	Main Com. Channel Direct traffic Build Community	Important Follow Opp. Leader, #-Listening	Responses/ Msgs, w/ easy, direct to email if more substantial	Responses/ Msgs, w/ easy, direct to email if more substantial	Main outlet for all content sources/ announcement	Back all Ent. Measures, extend reach, Channeling
Secondary communication driver (e.g. LinkedIn)	Com. Channel, Direct traffic Build Community Entertainment	Yes, as an extension of Twitter measures	Responses/ Msgs, w/ easy, direct to email if more substantial	Responses/ Msgs, w/ easy, direct to email if more substantial	Highly specialized business content	Pure business, thought leadership focus, more informative than entertainment
Communication & Entertainment driver (e.g. Facebook)	Com. Channel, direct to traffic Community building Entertainment	Yes, as an extension of Twitter measures	Responses/ Msgs, w/ easy, direct to email if more substantial	Responses/ Msgs, w/ easy, direct to email if more substantial	Second outlet for all content sources/ announcements	Main Entertainment Channel. Games, Fun, Engagement
Video Channel (e.g. YouTube, Vimeo...)	High-Quality Video Content-Source	No	Only when contact is made	No	Only via Video	Video support
Graphics Channel (e.g. Instagram, Flickr)	Picture Content Source	No	Only when contact is made	No	No	Picture support

📝 Workstream

A

Create a list of relevant channels and outlets where you will distribute messages about your product and your target audience. List the channels that are important for both your product and target audience. Narrow down that list to one or two channels that you will initially play in, plus another two, if they exist, where you just "listen" and gather information.

Just like on the social media channels, you must first listen and gather intelligence before you become active in the various communication channels.

For serious Public Relations (PR) efforts, contact your PR office or get some insights from an experienced and pragmatic PR expert.

Create a list of relevant channels and outlets where you will distribute messages about your company, its products, and your target audience.

Be aware that your products and your company may have different audiences depending how each is positioned. However, for the typical start-up the target audience of the company and the product is identical.

Once the company has launched more than one product or starts catering to more than one vertical, you'll have different target audiences; making a distinction between the company and the product is important when that happens.

List the channels that are important for both your product and target audience. Narrow down that list to one or two channels that you will initially play in, plus another two, if they exist, where you just "listen" and gather information.

Just like on the social media channels, you must first listen and gather intelligence before you become active in the various communication channels.

For serious Public Relations (PR) efforts, contact your PR office or get some insights from an experienced and pragmatic PR expert

Apply the Exercises for workstreams A and B. Carefully note the differences between putting a company versus a product at the forefront of your communications.

▶ Would you create your communications around a company or a product?

▶ Which channels would you use and why?

✏️ Key take aways

☑️ To Do

NYMA

Your Website(s)

Of all the communication channels available, your website is the only one you can truly own.

Your website allows you to present yourself, your company, and your product any way you like. There are no limits other than your ability and your budget. No other channel – not PR, social media, analysts, or any other outlet, gives you both the freedom and the responsibility to get it right. This is the point where it is okay to freak out for a second. Now read this: You do not have to create the perfect website in your first iteration. Just like you do with your product, you just constantly improve your web page. I will take a fail-fast approach over the never-get-it-done nightmare any day. The good news is there are some ground rules that will help you get it as right as possible from the start. I highly recommend Steve Krug's, "*Don't Make Me Think*," a masterpiece that discusses web design and usability. I have applied his theory many times in my professional life and have fared much better for it. Until you have a chance to read his book, what follows are some essentials based on my experience.

Product First

A full-grown website talks about all aspects of a company and its brands such as company philosophy, its history, career opportunities, executives on the team, financial topics, achievements, vision, mission, and, yes, product(s). However, make sure your product gets the most focus. Everything else is secondary to your product. There is nothing more important to talk about. It is also the thing that should be easy to present. All you need is a product description and a sales call to action that allows your customers to buy your product directly quickly and easily from your page, or points customers to where they can get it.

Okay, it is not that easy, and you may need a few more steps to produce the perfect product page, but here are the essentials:

- What is your product?

- Where can I buy your product?

- What is the price?

- What does the product (packaging) look like?

- Can I buy it online, subscribe to it, or do I have to find a retail outlet?

Do not Kill Your Business with Design

Web design is an easy and complicated topic. Keep it simple at first. Yes, it is great to have a fantastic design, but first you want to inform the audience and sell your product.

Here are a couple of key lessons for your first website:

- Have a clear structure.

- Do not kill your audience with endless amounts of copy or with a flood of pictures. Find a good mix.

- Supply a clear call-to-action. This can be buttons or text links, but buttons are much easier to follow.

- Highlight essential information for your users such as product description, price, and how-to-buy instructions

- If you have more descriptive or explanatory copy available for your users to dig deeper, create "more" / "find more information here" links or buttons that clearly guide your users to the other information.

- Videos rule! If you have a video that describes or explains your product, make sure it has a prominent place on your website. Use the call-to-action (CTA) features of video platforms like YouTube. This useful tool lets you add CTAs to the video, anywhere you want them. And this increases conversion rates.

Be Creative with Your Resources and Outsource Functions away from Your Website

If you want to keep your first website lean because you do not have the resources, it is okay to outsource some of the typical website functions to other places such as:

- Tumbler, WordPress, or the like as the architectural basis for your website. If you are more creative, format.com is also nice. You can find more providers like wix.com with a 2-minute online search.

- Twitter, for contact us and help/support.

- Facebook for "About Us" and/or to host legal disclaimers.

- Amazon as your sales page.

- YouTube for any video.

There are no fixed rules about how you should create your site other than some basic legal requirements and the European Union's GDPR. As such, make the most out of what you have within the boundaries of your objectives and strategy. A business-2-business (b2b) site would certainly require a more formal design than a consumer page with an under-29 target audience.

> **Hunt where the prey is!**

Finally, get your content as close to your audience as possible. Hosting a blog on a portal that serves your audience, as an example, will create many more views than channeling that audience away from their "natural habitat" and to your web page. Hunt where the prey is!

SEO/SEM: Keywords, Copy, and Messaging for Your Website

On order to have to your website ready for SEO (Search Engine Optimization)/SEM (Search Engine Marketing), the first and most crucial step is to use keywords and copy bits you created during the messaging matrix exercise.

- Website copy must hit keywords repeatedly to boost your SEO/SEM.

- Make sure any media you use is well prepared.

Customer Care/Support is Important

- Offer your users help! This should be a mix of FAQ's, supportive videos, or ways to contact your sales and customer care departments.

- Make sure you have customer care/support in place that can react quickly! A response that takes longer than one hour is too long. If you cannot respond that quickly, let customers know when to expect help. The absolute maximum is 24 hours!

- Be open to user-help-user forums. You do not have to host one on your website, use social channels such as Facebook (see the social media section for added guidance).

- Utilize automation for initial responses; e.g., "Thank you for your message. Our team will get back to you within 24 hours."

Analytics: Measure the Success of Your Site

When you measure your website's performance, you can improve the site and correct weaknesses. Points on website metrics:

- Learn where/how people come to your page, how long they stay, and which links they click.

- Good analytics are essential to constantly improve your page and identify shortcomings.

- Implement analytics tools such as Spring Metrics, Woopra, Clicky or Google Analytics, to name a few.

- Start with one of the free and basic tools that are easy to use. You do not need to go all-in and invest heavily in professional tools out of the Gartner report unless your organization is ready for it.

The Different and Most Common Types of Websites

When it is time to create your website, you must first decide what kind of page your company needs. Distinct types of web pages serve different purposes. Not every business needs each type of page.

If you already have an existing structure of pages and just need a web presence for a specific product or campaign, then go ahead and pick one of your existing pages. Then make sure you integrate the new page into your existing structure. Most importantly and as usual, keep your user in mind and offer a clear link to the support page.

In all other cases, reduce stress on your resources and create your first page around your product.

Your Website Must Generate Leads, or, Why Your Website Cannot Do It Alone.

Websites have changed significantly over the years. What started off as a pure source of information now generates revenue. It is hard to think of a website that is not designed to generate revenue for its owner in one way or the other. Companies today either sell products in online shops, sell advertising space, or use their website to generate and qualify leads.

Generate Leads

> **What started off as a pure source of information is now tasked to generate revenue.**

Every chief marketing officer (CMO) out there claims they drive tons of leads from their digital channels and all their sales teams must do is pick and convert them. "Like picking apples from an apple tree come late summer," or so they want you to believe. Although it is not that simple, it is true, websites and other digital properties have quickly become the most important channels for generating leads and sales across the business spectrum. A concert of social media, search engine marketing (SEM), and search engine optimization (SEO) for your website, videos, affiliate marketing, and online advertising are focused on driving more traffic to websites, contact sheets, or online shops with the single purpose of direct sales or collecting top-level leads

Because a growing number of Customer Success teams now give lead generating efforts a significant push, we will cover "Customer Success" later in this book.

Once you get traffic to your website, then conversion, the critical part of lead generation begins. What follows are a few simple tips to get you on the right track to a high-converting, lead-generating operation.

> Successful content marketing is the wiggling worm you cast in the sea to bait the fish.

Take your time. Do not try to short-cut the lead process and do not rush your visitors through the steps. You must build the five phases of lead generation into the backbone of all your activities. They are:

- **Awareness**

Lead qualification starts with relevant and attractive content. People who arrive on your site from your blog posts have already shown which topics are relevant to them. Your website and landing pages should focus on those relevant subjects to foster attention.

- **Interest**

Once your audience makes the step from your relevant content to your website or landing pages, you must make sure to keep them engaged by providing a) relevant content as mentioned and b) make the next steps as easy and intuitive as possible. As Steve Krug recommends, don't make me (your audience) think with crazy web design, too much information, or hidden links.**Trust** Allow your audience to learn about you, your team, and your company. Customers need to trust the people from whom they buy a product or a service. Know who your audience is and allow them to build trust in you, it is important. Help them get to know and trust you by telling them about your experience and expertise. Provide case studies for them to read up on, and, most importantly, present social references that are real people with pictures, names, companies, and stories.

- **Action**

Please don't make your audience figure things out for themselves. Remember Steve's advice. If your potential customers have to think about what to do next, they might end up thinking about that Netflix show they wanted to see, or the scarf they were supposed to order for a friend on Amazon.

Although it's nice your lead remembered the scarf, being a good friend makes them a badly converted lead or a customer not buying from you. Once the user is distracted, they exit your sales funnel. Have a clear call-to-action (CTA) that makes it easy for them to take the next step. Tell your users what to do next (e.g., fill in the contact form), but allow them autonomy to follow their own route by also offering email addresses or phone numbers to contact you. Your goal is to keep them in your sales funnel, taking steps toward a purchase.

- **Conversion**

When the user follows your call-to-action, make sure to thank them. The "Thank you page" is an essential part of lead generation and is a fantastic way to nurture this new contact. Thanking your new contact for following your CTA is also the perfect time to deepen your relationship with them, provide them with helpful information, and, while you are at it, upsell them to related products. Amazon does this best with their "other shoppers also found these products helpful / also purchased these products." Offer content they might be interested in, such as links to relevant blog posts, invite them to sign up for your email list, or to follow you on social media.

The Power of Landing Pages

Landing pages should be at the top of your lead generating activity list. Build them. Use them. Have plenty of them.

Landing pages are great because you can build and optimize them for just one topic or keyword. This laser-like focus makes qualifying your leads much easier because you already have an idea what your audience is interested in. Your blog post, the tweet, or the Google Ad — the trigger for your prospect to land on this page — allows you to focus all your steps. You can narrow in on the interests of your prospect to the point where everything they see speaks directly to them, right up to the conversion. Your nurturing and personalization will reach new heights.

> **Customers need to trust the people from whom they buy a product or a service.**

Therefore, do not be shy about having multiple landing pages. In fact, make them as focused as possible to make them as effective as possible. Once you have your audience on the landing page, follow the process described above.

Content Marketing and Distribution

Great content that offers value to your audience is the best way to get their attention. It also allows you to highlight your experience and expertise in a non-selling fashion. Successful content marketing is the wiggling worm you cast in the sea to bait the fish. Successful distribution of that content is the hook the worm is on.

This is where PR, social media, blogs, videos, and advertising comes in. Social media in concert with a well-written blog can be a powerful hook. It is inexpensive and can be easily focused, targeted, and customized. Well-executed social media is also interactive. See Chapter 10.9 to see how to build your social media operation.

Test. Test. Test.

You must test the quality of your landing pages, websites, or any other lead generation tool to have sustainable success. To know what makes one page more successful than the other, you must do a/b testing. This is the only way to gather enough experience with assorted designs, copy, or triggers to avoid accidental success paired with a lot of wasted effort on things that did not work. You must know what works and what did not and learn from the latter.

After you run tests you must then quickly convert what you learned into new efforts. Then, test variations again to further refine the quality of your emails or landing pages.

This is a process and circle of iterations. Yes, it seems like you are never quite done, but on the bright side, when you continue to work and refine, you have never quite failed.

VIII. Most Common Types of Websites

CORPORATE	• Basic company information for investors, partners, employees and general stakeholders

PRODUCT	• Often integrated into Corporate website, but especially in the consumer market and for large and very diverse groups, these pages are customer focused sales pages

INTERACTIVE	• Possible hub for all digital marketing efforts • Consumer facing page that combines social media with campaign messaging and channeling page to other pages like product, customer care or corporate

CAMPAIGN	• Short term, highly focused landing page for specific campaigns • Created to have single point of reference for communication channels • Integrated into main structure of either product or interactive pages • Provides means to measure success of a campaign

SUPPORT / CUSTOMER CARE	• Landing page for all support and customer care requests and topics • Usually features FAQ, message boards and contact details • User education like tutorials or manuals should be available here • Support / CC agents point users to this page for additional information

Key take aways

To Do

Notes

Social Media

Definition and Basic Workings of Social Media

When we talk about social media, it pays to make sure everyone understands the term. Social media is based on web applications built on the ideological and technical foundations of Web 2.0 (Kaplan and Haenlein, 2010). These applications allow users to create, share, and consume content via those Web 2.0 services without the traditional gatekeepers that in pre-social media days governed what content was publicized by, for example, newspaper, radio, or TV. Now, any user can publish her content to an unlimited number of users and connect directly with them and exchange information. Social media allows users to not only research desired topics, but also to share their feelings and express their opinions on any topic they choose, such as brands and their products and services (Tsimonis and Dimitriadis 2013). There are no boundaries that restrict the number of connections one user can make, nor are there limits to the extent or quality of those connections. With Web 2.0 and social media, the internet opened a new bidirectional information stream for all individual or organizational user. Users follow other users and like, comment on, or share another user's content. With this power, content can become viral because it can be shared by an unlimited number of users. Once information is published and shared by just one user, it can no longer be contained, and its originator has lost control.

> **Once information is published and shared by just one user, it can no longer be contained, and its originator has lost control.**

It is as crucial for employees throughout an organization as it is for private individuals to understand the basic workings of social media, its advantages, and its risks.

Social Media for Your Business

There is no point in asking, "Should a company engage in social media or not?" It is not a legitimate question anymore. If you are dealing with consumers on a scale in which they do not have to come to your store anymore and you do not know their names, social media is a must. The same is true for business customers, even though both their behavior and expectations are slightly different than a personal user. It is key to remember business users expect to get even more value from the content they digest than a personal consumer.

Users in Charge

Companies in the Web 2.0 age no longer own the information about their brand that is available online. Users now have the means to create content, comment on content generated by other users, and share what content they like. This shift toward a user-centric model has created a significant change in the way users handle available brand information. (Chari et. al. 2016)

According to Deloitte, 62% of U.S. consumers read brand recommendations online, 98% deem these endorsements trustworthy, and 80% reported the information affected their purchase intentions. (Pookulangara & Koesler, 2011, in Chari et al 2016)

Once your business is big enough to sell products beyond the local reach, you must think about using social media as a serious communication and interactive channel. Indeed, if your business is too small to reach customers who live 10 blocks away from you, a strong online presence with a robust ecommerce integration might be the only way to grow, depending on the kind of product or service you offer.

Your customers will look for ways to engage with you about product support, sales campaigns, or whether a product is available at a certain time, region, quantity, and much more. If you have a Facebook account, they will look for you on Twitter and miss you there. If you share your pictures via Twitter, they will ask you why you are not on Instagram. If you share videos, they will look for YouTube, Vimeo, Instagram, or Snapchat.

There will always be a new channel you do not have. Therefore, you need to regulate your social media engagement and educate users about your channels and their roles in your communications. Be prepared for your audience to ignore those regulations every so often and have a process in place that channels misguided users to the correct virtual location.

No matter how cumbersome this may sound, when it is time to decide yay or nay on social media, there's one point that should tip the scale in a positive decision. Whether you like it or not, your users already have a dialogue going about you and your products. They rate your products and services and encourage other potential customers to use them. Or, and this is the danger of not knowing what is said, some loud people discourage potential customers by revealing their unpleasant experience with you. If you are not checking your social media channels, everyone sees this but you. Now new customers will stay away and the number of returning customers declines. If you are present in this virtual environment, you can make sure you do not miss bad chatter as well as positive. You can react to it and influence perceptions. Change the dialogue to a trialogue which allows your users to engage in meaningful and mutually beneficial relationships (Tsimonis and Dimitriadis 2013). Thank those who post positive reviews and challenge bad ones. A business only has a chance to do this when it is an active member of the social media community.

"Yes" is therefore the only answer to the social media question, followed by "What, how, and where?"

Why Your Customers Use Social Media to Interact with You

When we explore ways to drive more interaction with customers, users, and fans, it is important to explore the motivations and drives that leads users to interact with brands, and why or when they grow into brand advocates and promoters. tThere are obvious motivations that lead to brand-related use of social media. We need to look deeper, however, if we want to figure out what it takes for a user to evolve from a consuming and passive user to an active participant and contributing fan of your brand's social media activities.

Social media is recognized as a platform on which people socialize, create boosted representations of themselves, provide help, or simply consume content. Although this is a drastically simplified description of the reasons people use social media, it gives us insights on how a brand could create hooks to guide a passive user into someone who comments, recommends, shares, or supports other users.

The step towards content creation is driven by entertainment, personal identity, integration, and social interaction, as well as personal empowerment (Muntinga et al, 2011, Saridakis et.al. 2016).

It is up to the social media content team to address all those motivations, and repeatedly. For example, a sublime message could be if a user becomes an active brand advocate, he can achieve his personal objective because you have enabled him to be helpful. If you allow your user base to create value for their immediate and secondary network by sharing your content, or even actively commenting on and making (positive) statements about your brand and your product, they can advance their social media status in relation to their circles.

This is a vital component that motivates your users to become active contributors to your brand's social media environment.

IX. Conceptual Model of Brand Related Social Media Use

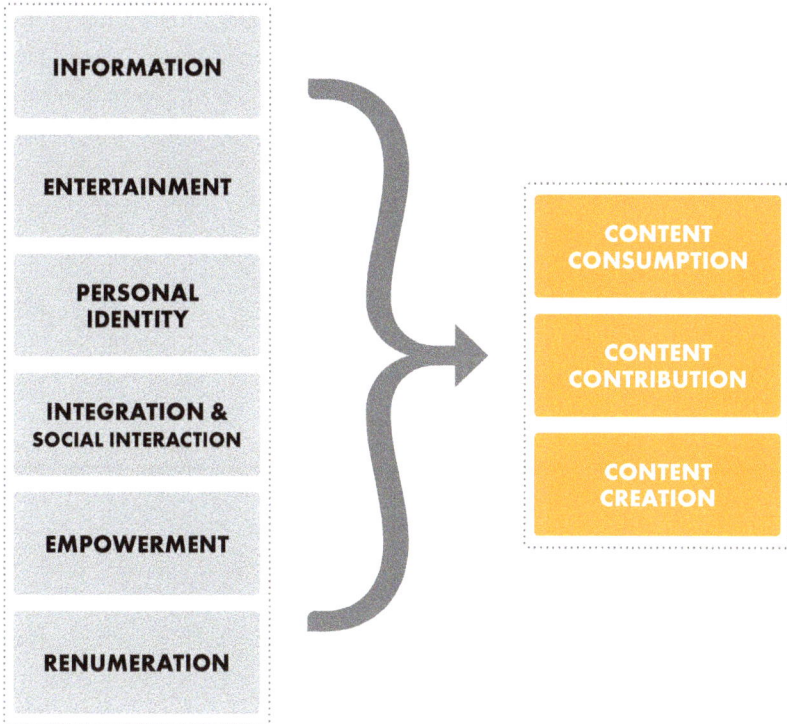

INFORMATION

ENTERTAINMENT

PERSONAL IDENTITY

INTEGRATION & SOCIAL INTERACTION

EMPOWERMENT

RENUMERATION

CONTENT CONSUMPTION

CONTENT CONTRIBUTION

CONTENT CREATION

Social Media: Strategy and Objectives

To get started with social media, just like anything in business, a list of clearly defined objectives should guide the entire team. The first point on the list should be: social media is not and cannot be an isolated tool. You should embed social media in your core marketing and communication strategy and use it to achieve the goals of that strategy. Once that is clear to everyone, define the social media goals and strategy.

The road to success in this channel leads through creating value, authenticity, and empathy for the user, or followers of the social media sphere.

> **Social media is not and cannot be an isolated tool.**

Social media is like no other channel. It supplies immediate feedback if consumers like or dislike a campaign, message, or product. Sure, there are people out there who never like a product, but when you measure the overall success of a social media campaign, it is clear to know whether the bubbly drink you deserve at the end of the night is champagne or sparkling water.

When you work with social media, you must remember once you publish the content, it cannot be unpublished. Sure, you can try to hide it or minimize the first distribution, but the more meaningful the content is, the harder it is to remove. It is a classic case of Murphey's Law. Because of this, there are certain safeguards you should take that will help you and your staff reduce inconvenient accidents. Measures such as defining an internal code of conduct, clear processes to deal with adverse events, and well-defined communication objectives, will ensure the success of your social media operation.

There are plenty of social media channels available that are different but do the same thing. Social media channels can be powerful and create a viral hype that transitions into the world of traditional PR. Just remember hype can be positive and negative. This is where the guidance from clearly defined rules and responsibilities comes in handy (Table X.)

Set S.M.A.R.T. Goals for your Social Media Operation

As I mentioned in the section about strategy and planning, there are many tools to choose from when it is time to tackle the various tasks you face when you start a business, launch a product, or tend to daily work.

One of my favorite tools is the "S.M.A.R.T. Goals" concept.

X.   S.M.A.R.T. Goals Concept

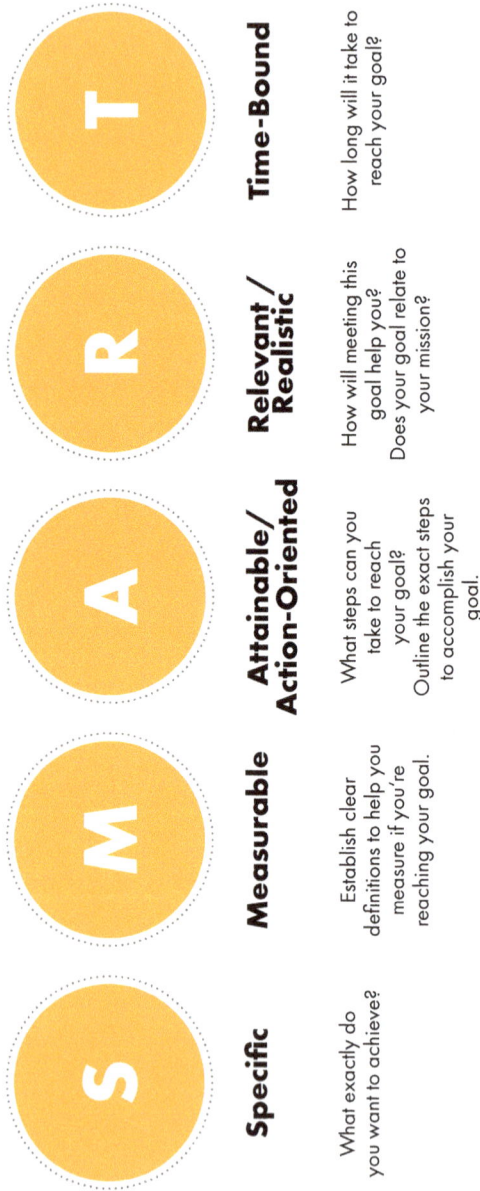

T

Time-Bound

How long will it take to reach your goal?

R

Relevant / Realistic

How will meeting this goal help you? Does your goal relate to your mission?

A

Attainable/ Action-Oriented

What steps can you take to reach your goal? Outline the exact steps to accomplish your goal.

M

Measurable

Establish clear definitions to help you measure if you're reaching your goal.

S

Specific

What exactly do you want to achieve?

Research proves companies with business leaders who formulate, document, and review clear and easy to understand goals have much higher success rates than those who do not. To measure the success of your activities, however, it is crucial to set a benchmark, or a starting point. You must note where you are when you start the effort. The benchmarks you set up should directly correlate to the goals you set for your company, your team, or just yourself. You will then set new easy-to-measure Key Performance Indicators (KPIs) based on those benchmarks. In the context of social media or digital marketing, those KPIs should be something like:

> Research proves companies with business leaders who formulate, document, and review clear and easy to understand goals have much higher success rates than those who do not.

- Number of visitors on your website

- Interactions with posts on your social media channels (likes, comments, shares, retweets, etc.)

- Growth of your direct audience (followers, likes of pages, subscriptions to newsletters or blogs)

- Potential for lead generation (Email subscriptions with double opt-in, contacts made per email, contact forms or direct messages per social media with product or service-related inquiries)

- All the above in the context of time (per hour, day, week, month, year) depending on the deadline for achieving your SMART goal

Finally, when you set your SMART goals for social media, you should also make sure you define clear steps to achieve your goals. Just defining your goals is not enough if you do not have a plan that outlines how to reach them.

This exercise will help you and your team get to the point.

Listen. React. Engage.

None of the social media channels will work right away. You must establish and nurture a following who will consume your messages and create interactions. Building a critical mass of followers to message should, therefore, be at the top of the social media to-do list. Being in a hurry does not help. Good things take time. Social media is a must-have for any business because the conversation about any product, yours, or the competition's, happens regardless of whether you take part. You will know what is happening in the online universe if you are part of social media.

The first thing that you must be aware of if you think you are going to create a social media strategy is, there is no such thing! Any social media strategy, just like PR, must be part of the general marketing communications strategy.

Social media does not function on an isolated playing field that you hand over to a couple of sub-25-year-olds. You must first get your marketing and communication objectives in place by breaking the plan down into channels, roles, and messaging objectives.

Three main steps will get you started in social media:

- Listen
- React
- Engage

Listen

As the word implies, this step focuses on a passive entry into the social media sphere. All you do is create channels and follow key opinion leaders in your business. However, this entails very thorough research for each channel. You can notice important topics and talking points specific to your space from your competition or opinion leaders. When you study important keywords and best practices in your industry, and analyze the conversations that are already taking place, you learn the rules and language spoken. You can gain important business intelligence that will guide you to the next steps.

Listen also means you search for your company, brand, and products to see what people are saying about them. This also helps define the strategy and will have an impact on the objectives you want to achieve. Your goal is to reinforce the positive perception of your brand and take careful action when and if you find negative comments. But really, at this stage, your mission is to listen to the channel to learn.

React

> Your goal now is to shape opinions and create themes that will establish a relationship with your followership.

Next, open the channels that lead to your customers. Listen to what your audience has to say and follow their conversations. Unless their conversations include incorrect facts about you or your product, or when users direct questions to you, you do not interact yet. This mode is still very passive, but also reactive. While you continue to collect business intelligence, you can now react to inquiries and start reducing the time it takes to resolve any problems. At this point, you will see a higher level of customer engagement with you and your brand simply because you are available. This creates a lot of responsibility for your organization. Clearly defined escalation processes should be in place as well as the code of conduct I mentioned earlier. How do you speak to your audience via social media? What social media persona do you want to communicate? How do you react? These are crucial elements of your social media strategy that you must define and rehearse. Anyone who runs the channels, from your CEO to your intern, must always internalize these rules and follow them. Not doing so can have dangerous consequences for your organization.

Granted, if you own the pizza parlor around the corner these decisions do not have the same impact as they may have in a highly regulated market such as tobacco, alcohol, or healthcare.

Engage

This final stage takes the most effort of the three. You are no longer just listening or reacting to what is directed at you, you actively distribute or push out content. You will start conversations and engage with your customers. It is at this stage that you begin thought leadership. Your goal now is to shape opinions and create themes that will establish a relationship with your followership.

This work is based on your predefined objectives and strategy. Every action you take must serve the objectives you set. These can range from pure reputation management to expanding the reach of your company and brand. Clearly defined processes with delineated roles and responsibilities within your team for each channel, and a well-managed communication and event plan for each channel, will define your success. You will now apply the earlier work you did segmenting and learning about your customers.

Social Media Channels

Now it is time to have a closer look at some of the most popular social media channels out there.

> With social media, more than any other tool, the user dictates how the game is played.

Not all channels are alike, as I have mentioned. Some are easy to start and others have advertising programs that can help you get followers quickly.

XI. Engagement Guide for Social Media

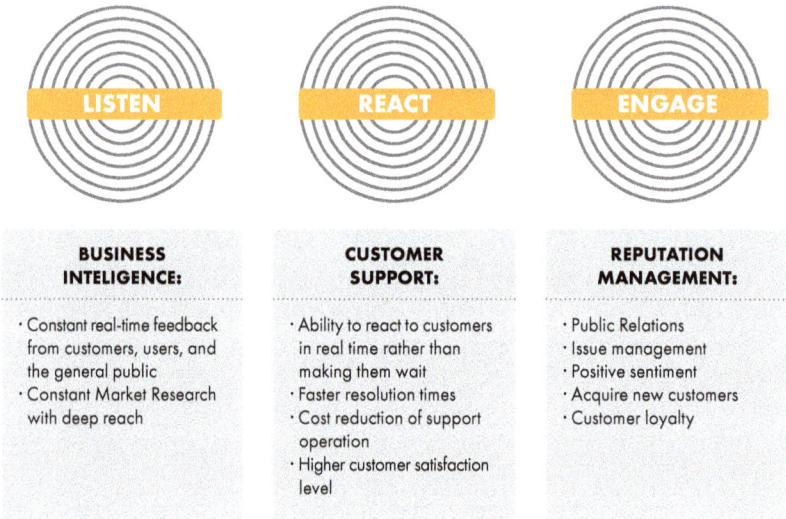

BUSINESS INTELIGENCE:

· Constant real-time feedback from customers, users, and the general public
· Constant Market Research with deep reach

CUSTOMER SUPPORT:

· Ability to react to customers in real time rather than making them wait
· Faster resolution times
· Cost reduction of support operation
· Higher customer satisfaction level

REPUTATION MANAGEMENT:

· Public Relations
· Issue management
· Positive sentiment
· Acquire new customers
· Customer loyalty

📖 Topic   **SMART Goals 10.9**

📑 Workstream

✏️ Key take aways

📋 To Do

XII. Social Media Channel Quick Look

FACEBOOK

Social Network

Business Features:
Company Pages
Analytics
Advertisement
Limited Branding

Specials:
Facebook Messenger
Instagram

Active Users:
2,06 BN

YOUTUBE

Social Network
Sharing Videos,
broadcasting

Business Features:
Company Pages
Analytics
Limited Branding

Specials:
High SEO, SEM and
Google Ranking
Impact
More Google
Network / Apps

Active Users:
1,50 BN

INSTAGRAM

Social Network for
sharing pictures,
videos

Business Features:
Company Pages
Analytics
Advertisement
Limited Branding

Specials:
Facebook
Facebook Messenger

Active Users:
700 M

GOOGLE +

Social Network

Business Features:
Company Pages
Limited Branding

Specials:
High SEO, SEM and
Google Ranking
Impact
More Google
Network / Apps

Active Users:
440 M*

TWITTER

Social Network for
sharing short messages /
micro blogging

Business Features:
Company Pages
Analytics
Advertisement
Branding

Specials:
Messages Limited to
240 characters

Active Users:
328 M

PINTEREST

Social Network for
marking / sharing
images and graphics,
ideas, information

Business Features:
Company Pages
Analytics
Advertisement
Limited Branding

Specials:
Digital Scrapbook

Active Users:
200 M

LINKEDIN

Social Network for
Professional Use
and Establishing
Business Relationships

Business Features:
Company Pages
Analytics
Advertisement
Limited Branding

Specials:
Very Strong HR and
Content Marketing
Platform

Active Users:
106 M

Twitter and Facebook are the channels traditionally used to build a following. Other channels let users contact you directly by communicating via your respective usernames. With social media, more than any other tool, the user dictates how the game is played. Although you decide how you present content, depending on the channel, the user always decides if she likes what she sees, if she will follow you, and which channel she prefers.

For example, you might want to only provide support through certain channels. Here is an example of when your users will quickly let you know they have different plans. Therefore, you must listen to and monitor all major channels, even though you may choose to push out communication exclusively on certain ones.

What follows is a list of the most popular channels to date.

WATCH OUT!
Before you continue reading know this: the list of channels could be outdated by the time this book is released. That is the hard truth about social media. Ask Justin Timberlake and Myspace about it.
Feel free to reach out to discuss with me the current channels. I would be happy to discuss the latest with you. My social handle is @moreeze (Twitter, Instagram) or just moreeze on the most popular channels out there.

Twitter

Twitter certainly is one of the most important channels in the social media universe. Its namesake short messages sent at high rates and succession can exert huge power or just be a blip in the sky. You can use Twitter to cross-promote activity of other channels (e.g. PR, Facebook, company blog), drive Twitter-specific messaging, or distribute pictures, videos, eBooks, and the like.

Because it is limited to 280 characters, Twitter is both focused and universally usable.

A big advantage of Twitter over other channels is it gives users the ability to search for related topics and join existing conversations. The hashtag or #-tag or just # has become a part of everyday written language. Users can comment on something or set a tone by adding a #-tag comment to their statement. #LikeThis The original way to use the #-tags in Twitter is to post a statement and tag certain keywords by adding the # in front of the word.

> A big advantage of Twitter over other channels is it gives users the ability to search for related topics and join existing conversations.

It is also possible to mention someone directly by adding their username marked with a '@' in front of it. My Twitter username is @moreeze. So, a tweet mentioning me and talking about a related topic could look like this:

Social media needs authentic messaging to be a success in #marketing #communication for #SaaS products. @moreeze

This is the time to mention that three #-tags per tweet are the sane limit. You can do more, but you should choose wisely. If every word of your tweet is important, none are important. Start over.

Those two tools, the #-tag, and the @-mention, give you the ability to engage key opinion leaders in your industry, or at least engage with their followers.

Build your Twitter channel organically; this means you must work the channel and supply meaningful content without buying followers or spending money on advertisements. Although buying ads and people to follow your channel works to bolster the numbers, it might not create the engaged followers you are looking for.

Once again, hard work pays off.

Facebook

Facebook, even more than Twitter, is the social character of social media. Facebook is used mostly for private purposes. Facebook members connect with family, friends, or people they went to school with or worked with long ago. The question, "I wonder what this or that guy is doing?" starts many searches on Facebook.

Facebook users also use the network to follow their preferred topics or engage with a brand. A Facebook campaign is like a Twitter campaign. With improved #-tagging capability, the mechanics work much like other social networks. People can decide not to be notified about something or when they are "mentioned" by someone, but that challenge is not unique to Facebook. It is no harder to build a followership organically on Facebook than on other social networks.

Facebook's advertising process is well-designed compared to Google AdWords, and their paid ads appear in search results or at the right-hand side of the result list.

Facebook, with two billion users who continually self-segment themselves, knows its participants well. Connections, locations, preferences, immediate plans, Facebook knows it all because it also uses external data sources to round out its knowledge about users. Facebook also makes it easy to run a cross-network campaign on Instagram. Although separate campaigns are possible, it is not necessary.

Added marketing and direct messaging opportunities are available through Facebook Messenger. This is comparable to an email campaign. A bot-like system interacts with users on demand and supplies them with links and helpful messages from you. Experts expect the platform will offer added tools via messaging functionality in the future. Facebook Messenger already has more than 1billion active users today.

What might be a bit scary or surprising from a privacy perspective is a pot of gold for those who want to build a targeted Facebook campaign. The segmentation, pre-built buyer personas, and messaging can work nicely for you. You can determine exactly whom you want to target and with what message. This focus allows you to see results even if you have a limited budget.

Facebook also provides a sophisticated analytics system that helps you make sense of the metrics beyond likes, comments, or shares.

Instagram

Instagram is a visual medium by nature. Users post pictures, videos, or any other visual media piece to share their message. The app allows users to easily stylize the images with either preset filters or a tool to enhance color, focus, contrast, and much more. "Everyone is a photographer now," is an often-heard sentiment since Instagram arrived on stage.

To use Instagram successfully, it is important for business leaders and marketing communication (MarCom) teams to learn about the channel and understand it. It's all about pictures and videos, not text. Instagram messages needs strong visuals to be effective. Posts must also follow the channel's strong demand for high-level aesthetics to be effective. Use Instagram to convey emotional and motivational messages and support a company's overall image. Companies like Nike, Mercedes-Benz, or Sephora are good examples of how to use Instagram successfully.

Instagram's ad engine is tightly connected to Facebook's.

Snapchat

Snapchat is a channel that is still changing. It started as a private channel on which users could send directly to other users' pictures and videos that self-delete after consumption. Teenagers left Facebook for Snapchat so they could chat secretly with each other without their parents tracking those conversations.

Users post a short picture or video message, add text to it and/or a theme and send this to their contacts either individually, or to a larger number of users.

Today, it is also a channel that has been discovered for commercial use. Many traditional media outlets use the channel to promote their stories or to give users backstage access. For example, the NBA uses Snapchat to supply behind the scenes footage of events. However, Snapchat took a blow when Facebook launched "Live," a live-video functionality that allows users like the NBA to broadcast videos live from an event. This may take market share from Snapchat, but at this point, it is not clear how they will react.

To use Snapchat, it is important for a business to have a user base. Otherwise, the content will not be visible to anyone. Therefore, businesses should delay the introduction of Snapchat to their active communication mix until they can move a large audience to the channel and have them become followers. This is crucial for the most effective and successful use of the channel.

Beyond that, the rules of authenticity apply just as they do on any other channel.

YouTube

YouTube is a unique and useful channel because it serves multiple purposes. As I mentioned, each channel in your social media arsenal needs predefined roles. YouTube can serve as a video content container that other channels point to, it can be its own powerful viral platform or, if videos are tagged and marked correctly, YouTube can support general SEO activity because its contents are prime targets for Google's bot.

I prefer to use YouTube for Customer Care and Support tutorials and onboarding videos. Publish all promotional videos and those that highlight product or services benefits on YouTube. To use YouTube's full SEO/SEM power, I strongly suggest you invest the time to select a good title, description, and tags for each video. You should also, of course, have different channels to address different genres, e.g., do not mix tutorial videos with advertising videos. Your users will not like that.

LinkedIn

LinkedIn is the obvious leader for targeting professionals. Companies use LinkedIn for their employees to gain sales leads and to find strategic partners or the next hire.

LinkedIn's clear business focus and active environment makes it a valuable platform. Users make connections quickly and can swiftly find, follow, and approach opinion leaders within a segment.

At this point, we still do not know the consequences of Microsoft's acquisition of LinkedIn. Things may change at LinkedIn, although that is not likely. Industry pundits expect LinkedIn will find its way into the MS universe and be highly integrated with other services such as Lync, Skype, OneDrive, and of course Outlook.com or Office365. That integration makes sense.

Pinterest

Pinterest works very differently from the other social networks described in this section. As on the other channels, you must show value to your potential "pinners," but Pinterest borders on overstating the value of standing out.

Nevertheless, Pinterest has a powerful community. A visual platform, you will usually find (product) pictures combined with short messages. Pinners pin an article they like to their boards and thereby share it with their community.

To be successful on Pinterest, as with most of the other networks, you must show value and communicate a strong marketing message about you or your products' strengths. You should also work with successful Pinners, called Super Pinners or Hyper Pinners, to gain traction. In short, you must invest in an opinion leader who creates word-of-mouth hype for you.

Organic growth on Pinterest is very time-consuming, resource-intensive, and demands an elevated level of creativity.

Blogs

Businesses owners and leaders across the board should be interested in blogs for two main reasons.

Writing your own blog enables you to position yourself as an opinion leader in your market or segment. It also shows your mindset. Writing blogs on a regular basis attracts other opinion leaders, interested parties, and followers. Well-written blogs can be powerful lead-generating tools if they are used right.

Running a blog also can be a very time-consuming activity. But done right, it pays handsome dividends eventually. Focused articles can be shared via other channels such as Twitter or Facebook where they act like a business card for you and your company. Your company blog, therefore, functions as a thought leadership outlet and a content repository like YouTube is for videos and Flickr for pictures. It is also a terrific way to support SEO (search engine optimization) and SEM (search engine marketing), functions. Use important keywords repeatedly throughout the content in a useful and non-intrusive manner, for a positive effect on Google rankings.

Third-party blogs are the second reason blogs are interesting. As a guest writer you can place your own articles on another blog and thereby extend your reach to new followers. Finally, use targeted blogs for online marketing.

There are two major blog platform providers that make creating a blog easy for any non-programmer.

WordPress

I mention WordPress first because it offers the most flexibility and is the easiest way to generate a professional-looking blog. There are many free themes, or styling templates, available for WordPress blogs and even more paid themes offered directly from WordPress and third-party providers. Finding the right theme is an easier decision than figuring out how to host the blog. Again, multiple options are available.

An effective way to start your blog endeavor is to use a free theme hosted by WordPress. A bigger challenge than your blog's design, however, is developing a strategy for the blog, creating the content, and keeping it fresh.

WordPress is an easy system to start. It allows you to easily expand, extend, and change hosting options. As blogs go, however, Tumblr is more of a social-network-type platform than WordPress.

Tumblr

Tumblr is a typical micro-blog, with an on-the-go blog platform. Although WordPress also supports mobile content generation, Tumblr does it naturally and with a more social approach. Tumblr has plenty of limitations though, especially if you want to host the blog yourself and adopt its look and feel to your company's website and corporate identity. No external platform is perfect, but it seems Tumblr is the less open version of the two.

Both blog providers offer the tools and tricks you need to get started. Keep in mind, as I mentioned, it is not the design that makes blogging a challenge.

Vimeo

Vimeo is the professional filmmaker version of YouTube. Vimeo users have different expectations than those who browse YouTube.

Many young or independent filmmakers use this channel to show off their work. It is also used as a model's set card or a graphic designer's portfolio.

I like to use Vimeo as a container for videos I use during specific campaigns, often accessed only with a special link. This way I can track the performance of the video better than relying on the much more public nature of YouTube. By using specific links, you get very precise metrics for that exact video. If you run multiple campaigns with the same video, it may not hurt to upload the same clip multiple times, so you have different links and measurements.

Vimeo is not a replacement for YouTube because it has no noteworthy influence on SEM or SEO and has a much smaller user base. Vimeo is a channel you use as an add-on or to house videos with a special purpose.

Flickr

Flickr is a great channel to use as a photo repository. It stores pictures which are hyperlinked or embedded into websites and blog posts or shared via Twitter or Facebook. Password-secured folders on Flickr are great for press kit materials.

Flickr, to a lesser extent, also has some viral powers, but it does not have the large numbers of users who browse and share pictures like they do videos of puppies on other channels. But, once someone has clicked on a picture or an album you linked from another channel, they will continue browsing if they find interesting content.

However, Flickr has been a part of the Yahoo! the universe for several years. With Yahoo's undetermined status, it is unclear what the future will hold for Flickr. The marriage with Yahoo! was clearly not a successful one and many users were angry they had to get Yahoo! IDs to access Flickr. As one of those angry users, I stopped using it. Flickr users are still out there, however, and the tool still has its purpose.

Only time will tell.

Communication Objectives and Roles for Social Media Channels

Various social media channels have different strengths and weaknesses, as I laid out in their descriptions. Matching the channels with your communication objectives is the next key step. Not all channels can have the same goal because the rules of engagement differ significantly within each of the channels (See Table XII).

Therefore, it makes sense to assign distinct roles to the respective channels you have chosen. Typical roles you can assign are:

Lead Communication Channel

The lead channel is the most important channel for your communication efforts. Twitter often plays this role; it is easy to position topics via Twitter and reach a target audience who either follows you, someone you mention, or a topic you mark with a #-tag. Because Twitter starts working for you on day one – followers or no followers – this channel should be your starting point.

Twitter is also a good primary communication channel because people are accustomed to reading headlines and then being channeled away to a secondary "location" on the web. This is common behavior and as such, it is an ideal characteristic for a primary communication channel.

Your lead communication channel is an entry point. You do not want people to get stuck there or consume all the information at once. Instead, you want to make sure this channel pulls people into your universe and leads them to browse your website or whatever content you offer via the link. Then you hope users share your content and your followers increase.

Secondary Communication Channel

A secondary channel usually offers a deeper glance into the story. Use channels like Facebook or LinkedIn for this. The secondary channel does not simply copy the message of the primary channel but puts a different or more extended spin on it. Although Twitter is limited to 280 characters, the secondary channel may allow you to use 500 to 2,000 characters, and graphics, videos, or presentations visible via thumbnails or larger previews to catch the attention of the potential audience.

If you make effective use of the number of characters available and leverage graphics capabilities, the secondary channel can tell the entire story without referring the reader to another destination. However, to achieve best results, stories distributed via this channel should always have a link or referral that allows the reader to consume even more details about your story. The longer your reader stays and the more locations she visits, or page impressions made, the more valuable the experience is for both parties. This channel should also support a return visit and opportunities for further engagement such as like, comment, share.

Entertainment / Tertiary Communication Channel

The entertainment and tertiary channels have yet another purpose. In many ways they can be used like and share most of the characteristics (number of characters, graphic/video inclusion) of the secondary channel, but their one, quite different goal is to engage the consumer of your content in a more entertaining way.

This is the main difference between the secondary and the entertainment channels. The latter is less serious and much more personable in its social approach. This channel is about more than hard facts and business news. It gives your company a human face behind the corporate façade. Who are the people behind your company and why should a potential customer of yours feel good about buying your product? These messages can infuse your handiwork with the emotions the product itself cannot give the user. Think of the late Steve Jobs of Apple and his vital role as the reason people bought and still buy Apple products. Much of it has nothing to do with the products themselves. Jobs gave Apple products character and his image transferred to them.

While not everybody is a Steve Jobs, it usually does not hurt to try and transfer that image. If you don't have a character in your company who can fit the bill, it would not hurt to create personas to use in advertisements and to serve as the face(s) of your product. Ronald McDonald certainly did not walk the streets, but his character worked well for the fast-food chain. Because of Ronald McDonald, consumers saw and related to the McDonald brand beyond food. In fact, his persona worked so well that it didn't take long for McDonald's to surround Ronald with an entire universe of characters.

Facebook and Instagram, or Pinterest to an extent, can play the role of the entertainment channel. It is especially important to make sure the job matches and fits the channel(s) you choose. The channel and how its native users navigate it will dictate how you should use it. Just stay true to yourself, your company, and the channel.

Repository Channels

Repository channels are video, graphics (pictures), or file (presentations) channels such as YouTube, Vimeo, Flickr, or SlideShare. They all have social components, especially YouTube, and they are great channels to use as a storage location for files. If want to reference a picture, load it onto Flickr and reference the link. It is easy to share SlideShare presentations on LinkedIn. These channels can help the company website and ease the webserver's load on bandwidth and storage.

Get Started with Social Media

Everything you have just read takes quite a bit of work and might seem like a bit too much at the start. Although you eventually must master all those skills to be successful, it makes sense to get your feet wet first.

Competitive Analysis

Before you do anything on social media, you must first research the competition. You can garner significant intelligence if you know how your competitors position their brands online, use social media channels, and interact with their customer base. It is important to learn from their successes and failures if you want to save time and money.

Create a S.W.O.T. analysis for each of your competitors' digital properties (webpages, social media, etc.) and take an honest look at what they are doing. What do you like or dislike? How does your competitors' audience react to their posts? Is the audience engaged? Is the engagement positive? You'll need to ask yourself these and more questions to analyze their online presence. This analysis will also reveal how your competitors communicate the benefits of their products and how they position them to their target audience. You can learn many lessons from this exercise that will help you distinguish your company, brand, and product from your competition.

> **Start slowly and remember to listen, react, and engage.**

Rules of Engagement - Guidance For Social Media

What follows are my tips and tricks for a successful social media operation.

Look at Your Target Audience and Follow Their Lead

You have created personas and refined them a couple of times. That is good. Keep doing that while you start your interaction with your audience. Now is the time to follow their lead. Your potential users will tell you which channels to choose. You can't play on all the platform, so have a look at the Channel Matrix and match that with your personas. Start slowly and remember to listen, react, and engage.

Find Your Voice and Be Yourself

How do you want to talk to your audience? Are you more formal or more of a friend? There are two essential factors that will tell you how you should communicate.

> Your content, and the value it creates for your audience will determine your success.

Your target audience is the first factor, as I mentioned! You want them to like you and interact with you. If you want to create a relationship with them, you must make sure they feel comfortable engaging with you.

You are the second factor – stay true to yourself. Be authentic when you talk to your customers so they can believe you. If you are not part of their age group, make sure you consult someone who is. Nothing is worse than a 40-year-old trying to use teenager slang. It just does not work. Don't try too hard or lose yourself in your effort to match your target audience. Get help or hold back a bit. At the end of the day, your content, and the value it creates for your audience will determine your success. This brings us to my next point.

Give Your Audience Value

Why should your audience like, follow, or engage with you instead of your competition or anyone else online? Yes, you are competing with everyone out there for the attention of your target audience, not just your competitors. You must create value if you want to attract fans on social media. Creating value does not mean you talk about your product non-stop. In fact, only two out of every 10 messages you post should be about your brand or product. The rest should be entertaining, informative, and helpful. Imagine you're on a long vacation with your friends. You must speak with them about a wide range of topics if you don't want to be the most boring friend ever. The same is true for conversations with your target audience. Do not be boring or self-centered, it is just not interesting.

Finally, make sure you really interact with your audience. If they post a question directly or indirectly, try to be a good friend and answer it. Never leave a question directed at you unanswered. Try not to overreact to messages you receive, no matter the content. If you want your audience to engage with you, you must engage in their communications to you. It's a two-way street!

You Are a Member of a New Social Group, Behave Accordingly

As a member, if not the leader of your social group, you must make sure you are a responsible member. Be active in your community and engaged in positive causes. Make sure these interests make sense for you and your brand. There should be a natural, authentic link and not something that appears created. Authenticity is the name of the social media game, and I will not tire of repeating it in this book.

If you are the funny member of a team and have a good sense of humor (politically correct), use it, you will increase audience engagement. People like to laugh and smiling naturally creates a positive chemical response in the body which creates a virtual bond with your audience.

Do not forget visual aids. Nobody wants to see one text message after another. If you enhance your message with graphics, pictures, or videos, you will see conversion rates increase significantly compared to text-only posts.

> Authenticity is the name of the social media game.

#-tags, Mentions and Other Tricks to Join and Start a Conversation

Imagine you post all kinds of nice content and nobody finds it. That is certainly not the scenario you want. You can avoid that outcome with active tagging and by mentioning key opinion leaders in your market. Unlike paid SEO, you can use the best keywords repeatedly and at no cost.

Start by searching for keywords. For example, if you are a web design agency, you would search for #web, #webdesign and for tools that you or leaders in the industry use. You will learn if those keywords make sense for you. If so, create posts that use these keywords. If not, try to find other words that are used with those in your initial search.

For example, when I first got in the 3-tag game, I started my search with "#marketing." From there it involved to #socialmedia, #contentmarketing, #digitalmarketing, and so on.

Don't be shy about it, but don't create posts that are #-tag nightmares such as:

In #digitalmarketing, you focus on creating #content for #twitter, #facebook and #instagram. #contentmarketing #socialmedia #marketing

This looks desperate and gives you a bad grade on authenticity. It is okay to use three to five #-tags. As for the example above, have a look at this:

In #digitalmarketing, you focus on creating #content for twitter, facebook, and Instagram. #socialmedia

Less is more. In the second example I focused #-tags on the most important and unique keywords. Everyone uses words like Facebook or Twitter, in many contexts. Strive to keep #-tags as customized to your brand as possible, but still allow a broad audience to find you.

Another way to get positive attention is to engage with leading people in your industry or get involved in conversations. If you use @ + their username you can message them directly, but for anyone to see. So, a message to me would look like:

'@moreeze: I have some more questions about building followers on my #socialmedia channels. Do you have more #socialmedia tips and tricks?'

If you message someone directly using her @name, her app will let her know directly. Also, anyone who searches for that person will find your direct message because you used her handle, her @name.

A painless way to join the conversation is to simply comment on an existing post. Particularly on Twitter, this allows you to join a conversation that is already underway and contribute to posts in your desired context. Of course, the same rules apply; add value to the conversation, enrich the discussion, and for goodness sake, don't heckle people. That does not build a good image.

Create a Complete Experience that Tells a Story and Features Events

Engaging your audience is not an easy task, but it is also not as complicated as you might fear. Have a look at the people or organizations you follow. Why do you follow them? Is it their brand reputation, the content they post, or how they keep your attention? Maybe it's all three.

Three popular Instagram profiles are good examples. All three accounts post pictures about and around New York City. All their posts feature high quality photography. Therefore, one would expect their performance is about the same. But it is not. All three accounts have a large following that many of us only dream of. All three are in fact premier profiles based on the number of followers they have and the quality of the content they post. Yet their performances differ quite a bit, which seems odd considering all three post pictures of the same city. What makes them so different that they achieve such disparate numbers per post?

Newyorkcity	– 1,640 posts, 1.4M followers = 854 followers p. post
Nyc	– 6,158 posts, 868K followers = 141 followers p. post
Newyork_instagram	– 2,693 posts, 1M followers = 371 followers p. post

When you dig into these accounts, you will see that newyorkcity tells a story around the pictures posted. The audience is captivated by the more personal touch of the account owner, and her numbers show it.

What does that mean for you? I encourage you to follow these accounts and study all three of them.

If you want to captivate your audience, strive to make more out of your posts. On Instagram, great pictures and information can get you to the upper echelon in number of followers. However, if combine these great pictures with personal stories around the picture-taking experience itself, the location, the motive, or what this made you think about, you will see a profound impact on audience engagement.

📖 Topic   Getting Started with Social Media

📝 Workstream

A B C

Before you post one word, set clear objectives. Do you want to:

▶ Increase your audience?

▶ Increase engagement with your audience?

▶ Establish a support/customer care channel?

▶ Establish a promotional and sales channel?

▶ Generate leads/build a sales funnel?

Key take aways

To Do

NYMA

Plan and Automate Your Postings

Now that you are ready to create the first posts across your channels, it is time to learn about the power of automation. To build a solid following and become an active member of the social media channel, it is crucial to post content regularly and at the right time.

You may have heard the truism, "timing is everything." It certainly applies on social media. This is a splendid example of why you made personas earlier in the process. Your personas will help you decide when the time is right to distribute content. When is your target audience most active? During which activity do you want to engage them? During school/work, or during leisure activities? Sure, you can try to manually post at the exact scheduled time, or you can use one of the handy tools available. Most of these automation tools offer free and paid versions. They all have different advantages or disadvantages. Play around with the free versions and figure out which serves you best.

Although automation is key to becoming a successful and professional social media manager, there are a few things you cannot and should not automate. You must plan regular times each day, or at least once or twice a week, to get out there into the virtual world and interact personally with your audience. As I mentioned, you are a member of a new group of "friends" now and you'll want to behave accordingly. During these automation and planning phases, it is just as important to plan "manual time." Schedule it and keep those meetings.

> Keep things sweet and simple, especially at the beginning of your social media activities.

There are plenty of automation tools out there. I encourage you to turn to a search engine and search for "top social media automation tools." That search will get you plenty of hits for the most popular tools and reviews at the time of your search. This is a fast-moving industry, so tools come and go.

The best way to approach automating your social media campaign is list what tasks you can automate and then to go out and find the right tools for each purpose, either via one or with a combination of tools.

Example of a Social Media Plan

Keep things sweet and simple, especially at the beginning of your social media activities. Sometimes that means using less complicated tools and going back to media (paper!) that gives you an overview you can stick to the wall.

An editorial schedule that makes sense of all your social media activities and an oversized printed version of said plan can be lifesavers. Here are some guidelines for your plan:

- Include all communication outlets and give each outlet enough lines to reflect (possibly) multiple postings per day.

- If you work in multiple regions with different languages, make sure to note the predefined languages.

- Use a color-coded legend for the distinct types of postings you want to automate. These can range from thought leadership content to straight informational postings to gamification, event reports, or statement posts. You will be able to better define post criteria as you gain experience, but it is crucial to be prepared to do it at this point.

- Do not shy away from entering the full post, or at least note a reference to a press release such as a link, in the plan's boxes. You need to be clear if you want to be successful.

Graphic XIII is an example of an editorial calendar I created for Open-Xchange when I set up their social media operation. Editorial calendars are a great tool. You can grasp the most key factors in the chart with a glance: Channel, category, language, and date. If daily timing is important and you want to track that, you can either make each day a double column entry in which you add a time to each post, or you can create triple rows for each channel (in addition, or complementary to what is described above) to reflect either exact time or day segments like morning, mid-day, and evening. This is something you will decide depending on how you reach your target audience. Follow their virtual lead and apply that intelligence to your editorial schedule.

Advantages of editorial calendars:

- An effortless way to stay on top of all outbound communications.

- Allow identification of holes in the schedule.

- Color coding helps create a healthy mix of corporate messages and social engagement posts.

- Facilitate internal communication of all social media activities within the company.

- Simplify communication between planning and execution staff.

XIII. Example of Editorial Plan for Social Media Channels

Channel	Language	Friday 06/01/12	Saturday 06/02/12	Sunday 06/03/12	Monday 06/04/12	Tuesday 06/05/12	Wednesday 06/06/12	Thursday 06/07/12	Friday 06/08/12
Twitter	English	News		(OX „Games")	OX Statments	Archive Blog	News	OX Statments	New Blog
	English	News			New Blog	News	OX Statments	Archive Blog	OX Statments
Facebook / Google +	English	News		OX „Games"	OX „Games"	OX Events	OX „Games"	News	OX Events
Tumblr (Blog)	English	5-10 Archive Blogs ready / 1-3 new Blogs ready			New Blog		Archive „pimped"		
Flickr (Pictures)	English								
YouTube (Video)	English								

Launch of new scheduled postings ←

Legend

- **Though Leadership** — Achieve Blog / New Blog
- **Inform** — Business/OX News on Products, developments etc
- **Convince** — OX Statements
- **Report** — OX Events
- **Entertain** — OX Games

✏️ Key take aways

☑️ To Do

NYMA

Follower and Friend Management

When you start managing your followers and friends remember this: Do not go crazy about the number of followers and friends you have. Yes, the number of followers you have tells you something about your potential audience, but it is not the whole story. Their activity and engagement level are much more important. This said, you still must manage your followers and friends.

> There is an unwritten rule that you follow people who follow you and, at the beginning, this is exactly what you need to do.

Especially if you start on Twitter you must be quite careful of your follower management. If you do not follow people back, it is they will unfollow you in time. There is an unwritten rule that you follow people who follow you and, at the beginning, this is exactly what you need to do. Should you become a prominent thought leader you will massage this further, but at first, this is an effective way to start. It is all about consistently growing your follower numbers and not losing followers right away.

You can streamline friend and follower management with a tool that gives you the ability to follow-back automatically, or to simplify the manual follow-back. As I mentioned, at the beginning I suggest you simply follow people back and monitor if they are actual users or if they are so-called bots that only post adult content or other spam. Any tool should also send your new followers an automated message that tells them you appreciate the follow. The message should change and evolve. Your message should also reflect any active campaigns you are running.

Answering private messages should not be automated. This does not go over well with followers. It is like sending only pre-written replies when a friend sends you a text or chat message.

Original Content Posting

Make sure you understand how to use the channels when you publish original content. For example, don't post a lengthy text on Twitter or a big corporate statement on Facebook.

It will be easier for you and your team to know which content you will publish through which channel when you use the right set of platforms and define their purpose. Reference Table VII to freshen-up on roles and responsibilities of the various channels. Once you have mastered this, you can then plan how and when to publish your content and how you will promote it across the various channels. The automation tool you use here should be able to post scheduled content on all your chosen channels. Keep looking until you find the right tool. It makes no sense to use multiple tools because that negates the original purpose of using a tool.

Content Curation

There is already a lot of content available that is interesting to you and your target audience. Collect and share this content with your target audience. Curating content is a good and low-effort way to provide interesting information while not talking about your own company. Also, when you share content from opinion leaders or important people in your market, you build a virtual bond with them. You can position your company with the choice of content you re-share.

There are many tools that help with content curation. It is especially important to pick one you can use from any device. To get the most benefit from a curation tool you should be able to browse content on the go and schedule a post with only a few clicks across multiple platforms. Some curation tools also allow you to manage your original content and cross-check timing, so you don't triple-post content. The keywords here are easy and comfortable. Only when it is easy and comfortable to browse and share available content will you do it on a regular basis. This is the time to remind you that it is crucially important to be a regular player in the social media arena.

Social Listening

This may sound like a small thing, but it is critical and worth repeating. As I mentioned in the Chapter, "Listen. React. Engage," a good way to start learning about your place in the social arena is to listen to what is said about companies, brands, or products like yours. You also want to know what consumers are already saying about you. You need to learn how your audience uses keywords that are important to you. For this, you should get one of the social listening tools that monitors your chosen keywords. Some of them even have sentiment filters which allow you to find positive or negative postings that include keywords you choose.

Strategically Grow Your Followers — Twitter, Instagram

As we have established, certain factors allow you to grow followers organically and others hamper that growth. However, it takes more active measure to increase your followers on Twitter or Instagram.

Again, the effort you invested when you made segments and working personas reveals itself as invaluable. Search for the key players in your market that your personas follow. Who are those people, what do they talk about in their own posts, and what hashtags do they use? Learn the language they use and how they engage their audience. Apply the knowledge I described in the *Social Listening* section. Once you have developed a feel for this, you can become an active player.

> **Learn the language they use and how they engage their audience.**

In addition to posting and using the right #-tags, @-communicating with key opinion leaders or other active players, joining conversations, and providing value, you also must actively grow your follower numbers. As I described in "*Follower and Friend Management*," one way to do that is to follow other people because they will most likely follow you back. Here is a tip: Only follow people who appear professional on Twitter. If they have less than 1,000 or 1,500 followers do not waste your time following them. Regular Twitter users reach a point where they are semi-professional actors who know the etiquette of following back. You also want to be aware of the stars and not follow them because they won't follow you back; they do not need to adhere to the etiquette. People follow Twitter stars because they offer so much value and their followers do not want to miss out.

Keep track of people by adding them to lists. This way you won't grow your following without any added benefit for you. Instead of clicking the follow button, you click on the little gear icon next to it and chose "Add / Remove from Lists." Here you create lists and add to them. These lists can be the stars from the entertainment or sports world you want to keep track of (in the event you don't have a personal twitter account), or you create lists that are closer to the task at hand. Name such lists "Follower Growth" or "Personalities" or "Social Media." Make sure your lists are not too general or you'll have a tough time finding anyone. But do not make them too detailed with only one or two people on them. These lists will help you dive into specific topics on demand.

When you have your working lists in place, you can look at the followers the stars or opinion leaders in your segment have. Those with between 2,000 and 50,000 followers are your perfect targets. Follow them and give them about two weeks to follow back. If they do, fine. If they don't, unfollow them. This is something you should do on a weekly basis, as it makes it easier to keep track of the people you have added or unfollowed. Do not add or unfollow more than 100 people in one session. This raises a flag by Twitter and may result in the suspension of your account. If you add 200 followers a day and unfollow 300 the next day, will get you on Twitter's bad side, so don't overdo it. This too, is part of being a good online citizen.

If you do this groundwork and produce a consistent stream of original content that provides value for your audience, the number of followers you have will grow. It takes time, but you will eventually get there.

The Right Tools for You

As with most things, it takes a little time to get a handle on how to use the different tools and figure out which of them is right for you. Don't make these choices lightly and do not shy away from booking a live demo. However, you learn about the tools best by using them, so don't worry about having exactly the right tool at the beginning as this will sort itself out. You may find yourself in a situation where a tool you've chosen is too much, too little, too expensive, or too complicated for you. If that happens, try something else, or venture into the digital world and ask questions, or start a poll. The results may surprise you. It also is an effective way to learn how to interact in the virtual social arena.

XIV. A List of Good Tools

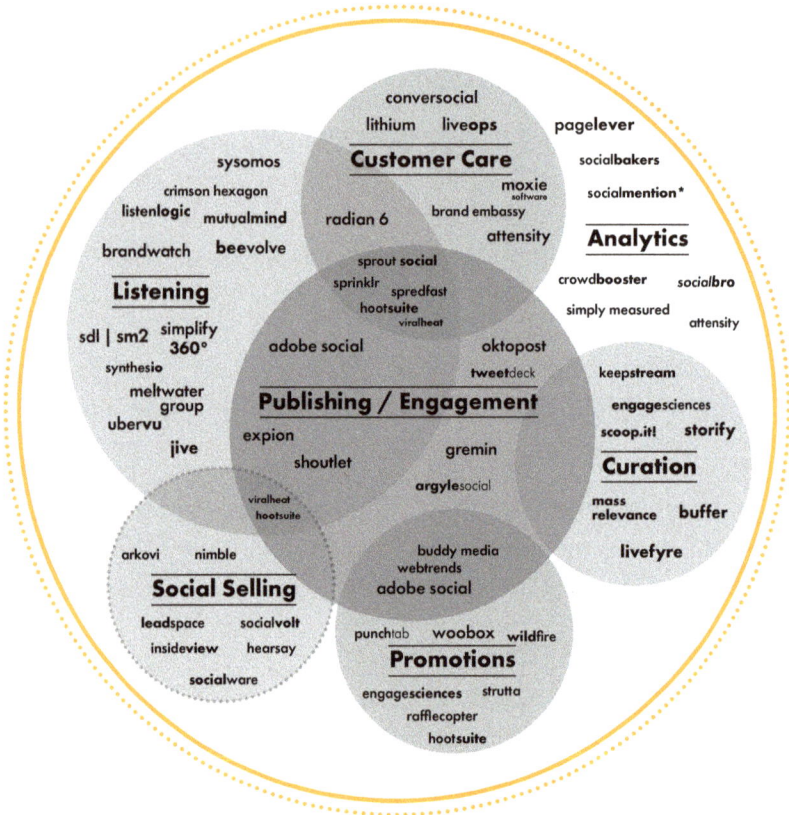

Customer Care
conversocial
lithium liveops
moxie software
brand embassy
radian 6
attensity
sprout social

Listening
sysomos
crimson hexagon
listenlogic mutualmind
brandwatch beevolve
sdl | sm2 simplify 360°
synthesio
meltwater group
ubervu
jive

Analytics
pagelever
socialbakers
socialmention*
crowdbooster socialbro
simply measured
attensity

Publishing / Engagement
sprinklr spredfast
hootsuite
viralheat
adobe social oktopost
tweetdeck
expion
shoutlet gremin
argylesocial
viralheat
hootsuite
buddy media
webtrends
adobe social

Curation
keepstream
engagesciences
scoop.it! storify
mass relevance buffer
livefyre

Social Selling
arkovi nimble
leadspace socialvolt
insideview hearsay
socialware

Promotions
punchtab woobox wildfire
engagesciences strutta
rafflecopter
hootsuite

Tools I Use and What I Use Them For Friend and Follower Management

- Tweepi – Follow/unfollow management

- Social Oomph – auto-reply, auto-follow

Original Content Posting

- Hootsuite – posts content on multiple platforms with manual or auto-timing

Content Curation

- buzzsumo.com – based on defined keywords, browsing content to re-share: limited free offer, plans start at +$79

- Google trends – a free content curation tool that finds trending online content

Social Listening

- Brand24 – monitor certain keywords, companies, and brands

Analytics

- Built-in analytics – free analytics tools offered by Twitter, Instagram, Facebook, or LinkedIn, to mention a few. These tools come free with the apps and are quite powerful. Have a good look at them before you spend a lot of money on paid solutions.

Honorable Mentions

- Canva – create images for social media; free with plans starting at $12.95/month

- Unsplash – a library of free professional photos

- Feedly – allows users to stay on top of certain influencers by curating their streams; free with plans starting at $5.41/months

- Buffer – multiple tools to manage your social accounts and automatic replies

📝 Workstream

Research "Best Social Media Tools" to find the current best tools. Social media tools change and evolve quickly. Tools that are useful and popular one day may be surpassed the next. As of 2021, I use hootsuite for myself and my company.

✏️ Key take aways

✅ To Do

-
-
-
-
-
-
-
-
-
-

NYMA

Winning Followers and Friends

There comes the point when all the theories fail, and you just do not know what to do. Your Twitter account has zero followers and now what?

Here are a couple of Dos and Don'ts when it comes time to build your audience.

Getting Followers on Twitter

When you are searching to find the right keywords, you will also find popular people who use those keywords. How many followers do they have? Browse their followers, are those the people who talk about the right topics or have the right descriptions in their profile? If so, follow them. All of them. After three or four weeks, browse those users and see who followed you back. Unfollow those who did not follow you. Then start over again. You will slowly build your number of followers. While the unfollow can be very, very cumbersome, you can use tools like Tweepi. Don't overdo it and only do this until you have a critical mass of about 1,000 followers on Twitter. Then let your content and solid work do the talking.

Ask Influencers for Their Support

You can always ask influencers in your market to help you out, give you a mention, or even suggest you/your brand to their audience. Some will do it for free, others for a fee. Like with paid postings, make sure it is worth it. It does not cost anything to ask, especially with respect, in a private message. Instagram is the channel where such an approach is most common and effective.

Enlist Your Family, Friends, and Colleagues

Ask the people closest to you to help by liking your page and content, especially on channels such as Facebook.

Do Not Buy Followers on Any Channel!

Buying followers will only hurt you in the mid- and long-term. For one thing, they are not real friends and followers, but deadstock who can only slow you down and shed a bad light on what you are trying to build. It is much better to work consistently and built your channels over time.

Paid Content and Promotions

All channels allow you to promote your content to a segmented target audience. This is also an effective way to accelerate the growth of your audience. It costs money, however, and thus requires a budget that can quickly climb to several hundred, if not thousands of dollars a month.

If you decide to pay to promote your content, it is important to set a budget for each individual outlet and across all channels for the entire campaign.

Conduct a/b testing to measure success rates. Book campaigns for a specific period and carefully monitor how the posts perform, and how many followers and friends you gain during the campaign and 4-6 weeks afterward. Experiment with promoting several types of posts and make your investment count. It might not be as good an investment to promote a basic status update as it would be to use the launch message for your new product, or a great press release you got on TechCrunch, or at least a very good blog post from your company blog. In short, be very selective when it comes to the topics you promote and make sure they offer the value to your audience you want to be known for.

> Be very selective when it comes to the topics you promote and make sure they offer the value to your audience you want to be known for.

Roles and Responsibilities within the Communications Team

One person alone should not try to manage the various channels and produce the content needed to drive a successful campaign. In an ideal world, you would have an entire team available to do the work. If that is not in the budget, at least make sure you have the minimum number of people necessary to do the work.

Successful Communication Starts at the Top

Regardless of the team headcount, you must cover certain elements if you want to run a successful communications campaign. You need to make sure you have full buy-in from leadership. If the CEO or top management does not support the communications strategy and the messaging it is based on, you will run into trouble.

Leadership also needs to communicate the messaging and strategy to all corners of your organization. This is traditionally the responsibility of the Head of Marketing or the person who holds the marketing lead. Once you have the support of leadership, you can consider the positions that could and should be filled. This clearly depends on your budget, your objectives, and the product you sell. The closer your product is to the social media universe, the better staffed you need to be in that department. Table XIV at the end of the chapter supplies an overview of a mid- to large-sized marketing operation. While some roles are not must-haves, there are three positions that are always required:

- Marketing Head
- PR Head
- Webmaster (design, programming)

It is inexpensive and valuable to have a freelance social media specialist to a) set up the first social media operation, b) create a social strategy, and c) manage the campaign. These are not necessarily full-time activities for a social media expert, so pricing should be manageable even for a smaller company. The more important social marketing is to your marketing campaign, the more critical it is to have a professional working these channels.

> The more important social marketing is to your marketing campaign, the more critical it is to have a professional working these channels.

You can fill other roles with freelancers who work either within a small hourly budget or on-demand, such as:

- Graphic designers, to support all communications with graphics and artwork,

- SEO/SEM specialists who optimize the website and make sure the messaging contains the right keywords,

- Copywriters for press releases, copy for the websites, or any other written communication published,

- Specialized PR agencies for either vertical (markets, products) or regions (international, different languages).

Communication is a Legal Situation

Every company today depends on its communications strategy, so it is important to have a communications policy in place. To create this policy, it takes legal representation familiar with your industry to clarify and define the Dos and Don'ts particular to that space.

Many markets and market segments have clearly defined regulations that prescribe what can be communicated to potential customers about a product or the competition. Breaking those rules can cause a heap of trouble you want to avoid. It is important to have any communication move cleared or at least evaluated by your legal advisors.

Get a specialist for this, not a divorce lawyer or the guy who handled your last home-purchase contract. As it is with hiring an accountant versus a tax accountant, the money you save will cost you ten-fold later when you pay to fix the mistakes.

If you think it's expensive to hire a professional, wait until you hire an amateur.

When a Good Party Goes Bad: Crisis Management

When is the last time you talked to someone and did not have to watch what you said, how you said it, or manage a bad reaction? I learned to pay close attention to how I spoke and interacted with others when I served in PsyOps where it was a matter of life and death. With corporate communications, it is not much different. How you react to negative feedback, complaints, or pure heckling is what makes or breaks a good marketing communication operation.

Communication in the digital arena is a two-way street. Before you shoot even a single message into the digital universe, there are basic but important steps you must follow to guarantee you are ready to receive and respond to the feedback that will undoubtedly come your way.

Your communications team should have a plan in place to deal with adverse events and your legal department must be involved in defining the process to manage those events. What is the plan of attack? How fast will you react? How will you react to various kinds of adverse events? You must handle customer complaints differently than a negative report in the press, or a heckler on an important multiplier board or channel. The first piece of information you need to react appropriately to such a report is to figure out where it was published. Was it in the press or on Twitter? Did an analyst report it or was it a random comment on Facebook? Was it just heckling, or constructive (if negative) feedback? The answers to those questions will define the proper reaction and timing.

> **Communicate a lot during good times, and even more during bad times.**

Two Key Crisis Communication Points

First, communicate a lot during good times, and even more during bad times. You do not want to look like you are hiding or even worse, hiding the truth.

And second, of course, customers come first! Should a customer have a complaint or reach out for support, reply ASAP. You do not have to produce a solution right away. Just letting them know you got their message and someone is dealing with it is a great first step. You should also let them know when you will be in touch again with more information. Do not make your customer wait around until you decide to respond.

XV. Example of a MarCom Team Structure

Title	Role in Company	Responsibility on Communications Team
VP Marketing	Global Marketing	Marketing and communications strategy, final edit of all content published
Director PR	PR	Responsible for all PR communications, works closely with Social Media specialists, provides content for social media
Marketing Team Member 1	General Marketing (Graphics, Video, Agency Management)	Depending on team structure: supports team, provides content, graphics, or research for content creation
Marketing Team Member 2	Event Responsibilities	Provides content in form of events to watch or attend, announcements about events, reports from events
PR Agency	External Specialists for PR	Sometimes hired to cover certain regions or verticals, support with copy and editing
Social Freelancer	Social Specialist	Manages all social accounts, translates content provided by the team into social-fit messages, responsible for campaign management (planning and execution), works closely with all other functions
Webmaster	Webmaster for Website, Blog	Webmaster for website and company blog, establishes look and feel of social accounts when possible
Additional Freelancer (e.g. graphic design, copywriter, SEO/SEM specialist	Various roles depending on need and requirements	Specialists for various parts of communications and its optimization help achieve professionalism

Create an escalation plan for adverse events. Answer these questions:

▶ Who will react, and how, to bad news, customer claims, negative press, or an incident on social media?

▶ What is your policy?

▶ What are the potential legal implications?

Create a plan that addresses the 5 most troubling incidents that could happen for a product like yours, and address each with a full action and communication strategy.

When an adverse events happen, you need a plan like this in place to help you stay in control and prevent damage to your reputation.

Key take aways

To Do

Prepare and Execute the Launch

It is time to bring it all together. You have done the ground-work and are ready to go. You may wonder, how do you put all this theory into action that will lead to a successful launch of your campaign or product introduction?

To cut to the chase, you need another plan; an overview that organizes the tasks at hand and recognizes interde-pendencies, production, delivery, announcement, and re-action times, and much more.

Any good launch plan has distinct phases that depend on the scale and scope of the launch. It is helpful to be aware of the plan's phases ahead of time.

Before the Launch Plan

Kick-off / Planning / Scope

- Look at the strategy and the objectives and define what constitutes a successful launch.

- Start with your preferred launch date and work back to a kick-off time. Does that timing work? What are the crucial factors that will make your launch suc-cessful? Which of those factors will take the most time in the pre-launch phase?

- Note of advice: Add 25% more time than you think everything will take. The rule is, if you are pressed for time, things will go wrong. Everything takes lon-ger. Sometimes things just go wrong and you have to change plans. If your schedule is too tight, every minor delay puts the launch in jeopardy and hurts your project.

- Every minute you waste at the beginning will cost you hours at the end.

- Do not get caught by surprise, plan.

- It is nice to plan when you have unlimited financial resources and an opulent budget. Unfortunately, for most of us, reality looks quite a bit different. We must make the most out of the budget we have and squeeze it to make it work.

> **Sometimes cheap is the most expensive thing you can buy!**

Good planning and scoping out your project are financial necessities. An out-of-control project means one thing; the budget will blow-up in your face. Costs increase when you must do things over or in a rush.

Thorough planning and good research into vendors and suppliers will help a lot. But be careful, sometimes cheap is the most expensive thing you can buy!

Communication Rules

- Communication Rule 1: Your teams must speak with each other and be aware of each other's processes. Compartmentalization is okay, but it can hurt you when team members need to know the big picture. Your team will be most effective if everyone is aware of how their work fits into the overall plan and which steps depend on their performance. Therefore, set a baseline communication rule that everyone is aware of and understands.

- Communication Rule 2: We all know what happens when we assume, don't we? Assume = makes an **A$$** out of yo**u** and **me**! This adage is especially true in project work. Make sure you and your team do not take any, not even a tiny bit of information, for granted. Instead, encourage them to ask too many questions and verify a tidbit once too often. Not speaking up is the first step to trouble.

- Communication Rule 3: Communicating also means receiving information. Just because someone has communicated something does not mean anyone received, heard, or understood it. Communication is only successful when that happens.

- Communication Rule 4: Communicate issues early and openly. If you don't let someone know you may be in trouble or need help, you pass up the opportunity for the team to help prevent an issue.

- Communication Rule 5: Communicating with your customers is tricky. You should not lie to your customers at any time. However, sometimes, managing communication and finding the right words makes a world of difference. If your team is young and you don't know how people might perform in front of a customer, conduct some role-playing. Learn to communicate as a team. There are many ways to say something, but your presentation to your customers should always be professional.

Preparation / Vendor Briefing / Iterations

- There will be items in your plan that need preparation/production time. Make sure you plan for this.

- Brief your vendors and verify they understand what they must complete and in what timeframe. The more complex the task, the longer it will take to prepare a vendor. If you have worked with the production team before, it will go faster than it will with new vendors. Make sure they understand what you expect of them.

- Make sure you also factor in production time for re-iterations. Not every first draft will be spot on. Be prepared to have multiple iterations before you get the right results.

- The iterative process can be even longer if you are printing something because the printer may have to send you a hard copy proof. Be ready for shipping delays.

- If you're creating a campaign/product landing page:

Domain
You got your domain, right? If not, make sure it is available and reserve it. It would be a shame if the wrong URL is on all your online, print, or video collateral.

Server
Make sure your server has the bandwidth and capacity to deal with your launch. Be realistic, but also have some buffer. If you aren't Apple, you may not need your own multiple data centers. However, the server in your closet may not be the best choice. What if you lose power because the dog chews through your cable? You should have an elevated level of professionalism around such a crucial item like your website. Many hosting companies have some good offers.

Production

- People often forget they must produce everything they use first. The production of most things is more complex and takes more time than one initially thinks.

- Production of print material: You must create and license both graphics and copy before the actual print production can start. This usually takes longer than the actual production itself. Plan accordingly.

- Video production/Animation vs. real-life video: You can usually produce animation more cost-effectively and faster than real-life video. There are situations however, where a mix makes a much better product. If so, be ready for the extra costs which will stem mostly for the extra time this takes. If you film people, do not forget to get them to sign a waiver that allows you to include them in your video.

Storyboards: Take your time to get a good script and storyboard in place. This will avoid surprises when you see your first layout.

Voiceover: Of you use a video with voiceover, approve the script before you head to the studio to record.

Music: Make sure you license the music you're going to use in your video. Non-commercial use is viewed leniently, but commercial use is easy to discern and potentially very costly. Free or low-cost music is available through many platforms such as premiumbeat.com or shutterstock.com to name a few.

Cost-efficient video production: There are many video producers who can do a decent job on a budget. You don't always have to spend thousands of dollars to get a decent video. Explore the world of alternative video production, it can save you a lot of time and money.

- Website: Everything I explained about print collateral and video applies to your web presence, only twice as much. Beyond worrying about the basic process of creating your website, you must ensure the site works on multiple browsers, devices, and so on. As such, complete your website well before your launch date. Murphey's law is best friends with the bug that hits the eve of your launch.

Implementation and Set-Up

- Once you've produced communications, they are ready to serve you. Use automation to help you coordinate and time the publishing of your messages on the various channels. Arranging the automation also takes time, depending on the volume and complexity of your communications plan. Be careful when you organize your automated messages; you don't want to mix up orders or channels.

- Do you have to physically ship anything? If so, this is when you should make sure the shipping services/vendors are in place.

Launch, Execution, and Monitoring

- It is crucial to have a test launch a few days ahead of time.

  - Does the automation work?

  - Is your website up and ready?

  - Is all the collateral ready?

  - Do you have people in place during the actual launch who can fix whatever issues may occur?

- It's all-hands-on-deck!

- Throughout the launch, monitor all your communications and be on the lookout for feedback and comments on social media and from PR outlets. There are tools that can track keywords for you.

- If customers, users, or opinion leaders have a question, be ready to answer.

- Should there be an issue, address it ASAP and be prepared to launch communications around issues that are serious.

Post-Launch and Review

- This is the time to address issues that may have occurred during the launch.

- Actively reach out to your customers or users to gather intel about how they are doing with your product. You can use this intel in several ways.

  - If you learn that users of your software have problems onboarding, you may want to create educational or tutorial materials to address the issues.

  - If you have customers who are super happy with what you are doing, why not turn them into testimonials and use this during a second wave of communications?

Create the Launch Plan

There are plenty of tools available to help you create your launch plan. Do an online search for "project plan tools" and you will find tools to help and sites that recommend and compare tools.

If you do not have a project planning tool however, and don't want to learn something new, a spreadsheet will also work. You should be honest about the complexity of your project and the number of participants when you make this decision. If you are just a few people with basic needs, it is fine to use a basic spreadsheet. The advantage of using a spreadsheet is most people have access to either Excel, OX Spreadsheet, or Open Office.

Start with a basic layout and expand it from there. Create it in a way that allows you to expand the number of action items as needed. Create timelines for each action item. If you do not know the timelines, contact your subject matter experts or vendors to get an estimate. Ask them for best- and worst-case estimates.

📖 **Topic** Production

📝 **Workstream**

A B C

Download a collateral production plan at nycmarketingacademy. com. Platforms like Fiverr are very helpful if you're on a low-budget.

✏️ **Key take aways**

☑️ **To Do**

-
-
-
-
-
-
-
-
-
-

NYMA

But Wait,
There's More

By now, you have everything you need and are well-equipped to start your marketing campaign, operation, or the go-to-market of your brand or product. You can jump a few pages ahead and dive right into the exercises.

However, if you are a bit further along in the process and are in touch with current customers and users, it is time to manage and perfect those interactions. If you are ready to take your customer relationships to the next level, continue with the Customer Success chapter that follows.

> **The success of your company depends on the success of your users or customers.**

The Customer Success section is a compressed entry on a topic that is so crucial to business success it could fill an entire book.

Enjoy reading what could be a preview to more, and feel free to reach out to me should you have questions.

Customer Success: Your Success Depends on It

Although the idea of Customer Success (CS) is not completely new, it is getting more attention from business leaders lately. The underlying philosophy of Customer Success is the success of your company depends on the success of your users or customers. If they have a tough time using your product, you will have a challenging time keeping them, and you certainly will not get return business.

To make your customers successful, you need to have important intelligence about their demographics, their user behavior, and what they hope to achieve by using your product. You must gather customer intelligence. How do they use your product? How do they interact with your brand and company, with your customer support structure? As I never tire of reminding anyone who will listen, you must know your customer. This intelligence drives success.

Customer Success is a term used mostly in the software business, especially in Software-as-a-Service (SaaS), where the implications of healthy relationships, churn rates, and support volume have an immediate impact on the bottom line. All businesses, with or without subscription models, that want return business must engage in customer success activities.

> **Customer Success is an essential business function within an organization and should be part of its DNA.**

To understand what makes your customers successful you must understand their desired outcome. This requires a good understanding of what your customers a) do with your product today and b) might need in the future, as well as, and this might be most important, c) the context in which they use your product. Why do they use your product? What do they hope to achieve with it? To learn these things, you need to interact with your customers. Meaningful interactions with your customers that yields insights, requires that you have a relationship with them. Although that might seem intense, it is always worth the effort.

Customer success is also at the core of what makes your business a robust growth company. A good CS operation can reduce Customer Acquisition Costs (CAC), increase customer Lifetime Value (LTV) or Average Revenue Per User (ARPU), and at the same time reduce churn rate.

Especially in SaaS businesses, the initial CAC can far outweigh customer revenue during that customer's first 6-12 months. In extremely competitive markets, a vendor may not even make a profit until the customer renews her subscription. The ability to control your churn rates and increase the contract value, or the share of wallet (different terms for ARPU), of a subscriber, is crucial to the sustainability of your business.

As such, Customer Success is an essential business function within an organization and should be part of its DNA. (Murphy and McClafferty 2016)

Know Your Customers Desired Outcome

There are few growth factors as important as the following:

- Convert existing customers to repeat buyers or subscribers,

- Reduce churn by increasing customer happiness and reducing the number of one-time buyers.

Yes, winning new customers is important, but if you cannot keep them and increase your share of wallet, you will drain your resources. Companies that convert customers into returning customers see a significant increase in LTV per customer. As illustrated in Graphic XVI, the first sale is only part of the overall potential customer revenue. Therefore, why not simply convert all customers into regular customers? What does it take to make this happen?

XVI. Customer Revenue Potential

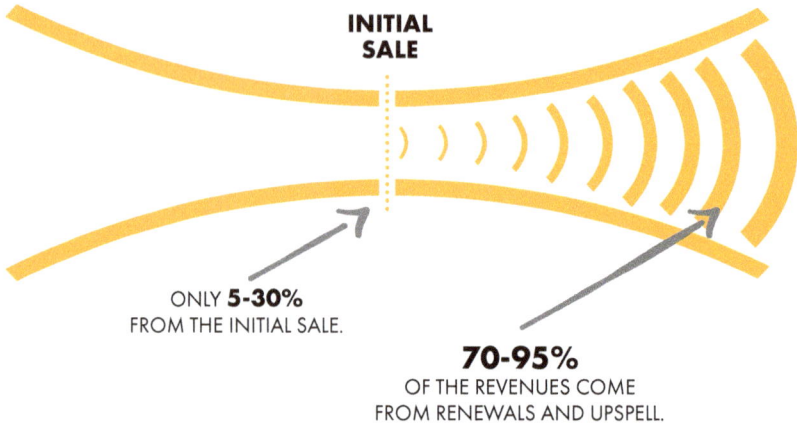

INITIAL SALE

ONLY **5-30%** FROM THE INITIAL SALE.

70-95% OF THE REVENUES COME FROM RENEWALS AND UPSPELL.

The answer is as easy as it is challenging; you just need to know what the customer wants to buy next.

To develop the insight necessary to answer that question, you must learn a few more things about your users, such as:

- How did she become a customer of your company in the first place?

- What does the customer want to achieve with your product? What was her desired outcome when she made the purchase or subscribed to your service?

- Are there follow-up services that could help her achieve even more?

- What are the mid- and long-term requirements of your customer and can your company support them?

Customer Success in Your Company

A good customer success program is involved in all aspects of your company: marketing, sales, product development, and of course, support or customer care. Effective customer success operations serve as the liaison between customers and the company and strive to create value for both sides (Customer Success Association, 2016).

Although the CS team is responsible for a variety of tasks, , one of their major responsibilities is to gain robust data about customers and users which then contributes to company-wide user intelligence. The data collected is comprised of the customer experience during the sales cycle and user behavior and experiences with the product or company.

The CS team collects, analyzes, and in partnership with the respective departments, acts on the data to improve the overall user experience with your company, brand, product, or service.

This information can lead to product changes to discuss, design, test, and then apply or not apply, depending on the outcome of the tests. The CS team also works with marketing and product marketing to create user education materials, so customers have a better first experience with a new product or service. Successful onboarding, that is the initial set-up and a customer's opening period of use, defines the customer's attitude for the rest of the contract or product lifecycle. As such, you cannot over-invest in a quick and seamless onboarding experience. Your user will decide in those crucial first minutes whether to become a promoter or detractor on your Net Promoter Score (NPS). It is extremely tough to change a detractor into a promoter and it requires a lot of resources. Luckily, when managed properly, a promoter can be quite forgiving should things go wrong. Open and transparent communication together with clever relationship management can save promoters.

> You cannot over-invest in a quick and seamless onboarding experience.

Key take aways

To Do

NYMA

Customer Success: A Scientific Approach

Measuring the success or happiness of your customers has always been a numbers game. Even the owner of the corner hardware store knew exactly how his customer base was doing because he talked and had a relationship with them. This is how he evaluated if his customer, John Smith, was happy or needed anything else from his store. He would notice and mention to Elizabeth Johnson that she had not been around for a while and inquire if everything was okay. While this does not sound very scientific, it is a very grassroots form of customer-focused research.

Digitalization of almost every product and service available in 2021 allows entrepreneurs to use precise analytics to be more scientific in their approach to assessing the success of their businesses. If there is one thing we have learned since the launch of search engines, SEO, customer relationship management (CRM), and the like, it is data and the ability to collect, visualize, analyze, and convert the results into actionable outcomes is the new gold. As I may have mentioned, data is the heart of our economy and your business success.

> Data is the heart of our economy and your business success.

Your CS operation should be the source of all the customer-related data collected. You should collect and analyze CRM data, product-integrated user behavior measures, and communication analytics that measure all inbound and outbound customer communication. A company-wide task, the CS team should lead or be heavily involved in collecting these metrics.

A metrics- and data-driven approach to CS is crucial to understanding your customers based on objective data. Results of soft research rounds-off the results of the constant probe into the mind of your customers.

Measure. Collect. Ask. Test. Start Over.

There are many ways to gather the important data that will help you:

- Talk to your customers and ask them for feedback, insights, and to help you improve how you serve them.

- Learn about your customers and prospects and get to know them,

- Analyze their behavior around your digital properties or within your product,

- Collect feedback about your service, products, staff, and company,

- Measure effectiveness of your communication, marketing, sales, and your customer care and support efforts.

- Ensure your data sets are as complete as possible. Any blind spot, or something you've missed, could distort your results, and have negative impact.

Although this is a lengthy list of activities, the most important thing is to start, then refine and improve it as you go. Never stop collecting and analyzing data from as many vantage points as possible; this will make you less vulnerable to data blind spots.

What follows are a few basic ways to measure your success and collect data.

Analytics

Analytics can draw metrics from the following data points:

Your Product

If you sell a digital product of any kind, you should consider integrating an analytics system in the product. The system should not target private details about your users, but educate you about user behavior within your product. How often is the product used? What is the user journey through the product? Which modules or features are used more, and which are used less? Does your user onboarding work? Do users even find it? You can learn this and much more from product/user analytics.

Website

> Your users will tell you what they like or dislike, you just need to ask them.

There are many tools available to help you understand your website audience. The mix of how many users visit your page and the duration of time they spend there will provide you with a lot of valuable insights. It will help you refine the effectiveness of each page and streamline how users find the desired content, and which content users want in the first place. Measuring where your audience comes from enables you to learn about traffic sources so you can optimize efforts to channel your audience to your websites or landing pages.

Social Media networks and blogs

These platforms all supply a great deal of built-in integrated analytic tools. Utilizing other (free) tools to plan and track your posts and links will give you a deeper grasp of how these platforms can work for you.

Customer Feedback

You have an opportunity to ask for feedback after every customer interaction. That doesn't necessarily mean you should put a ten-page survey in front of users every time they visit your website, but a quick survey, star-based rating, or a poll on your digital properties can give you a lot of information. These techniques are just as important as random follow-up emails or calling a customer after an interaction with a sales or customer care / support agent. Your users will tell you what they like or dislike, you just need to ask them. Do not just ask five users. Handy research tools such as survey monkey have helpful articles like this one: https://help.surveymonkey.com/articles/en/kb/How-many-respondents-do-I-need

to help you determine how many responses you need to get meaningful results.

Surveys

In addition to the data you get from quick feedback as I described above, comprehensive customer surveys also supply key intelligence. Ask your customers to supply information about demographics and their level of satisfaction. Include specific questions about your market and your product or your competitors' products. Do not do this more than two or three times annually, and if you send multiple questionnaires a year, ask different questions that focus on a unique topic each time you reach out.

Offer incentives that will motivate your customers to take part. To avoid sanitizing the data, carefully consider the questions you pose and the users who receive the survey. Do not ask leading questions and make sure your group of participants is not biased.

Polls

Polls, especially very quick ones, help you measure the pulse of your audience and customers. I find them most effective if they are an either/or poll that includes a follow-up question that clarifies their choice. These polls, like quick customer feedback sliders on a website, can provide data points to drive decisions on design, feature choices, or product ranges.

Social Media

Social media is an inexpensive and highly effective tool that allows you to reach a greater audience than you ever could through direct contact or your website alone. You can distribute surveys, feedback requests, and polls through social media networks and the channels your target audience uses.

Incentives for participation helps increase the volume of people you reach, but make sure the incentive gives your audience value or it will backfire.

Your Customer: The Most Important Data Point

All the data-driven marketing we do today sometimes feels like we are using a bazooka to shoot birds, which you obviously shouldn't do in the first place. If you are a small business like the corner bike shop in your neighborhood, or the local flower store, or even a small coffee roasting company in the German countryside, like friends of mine, you may still know your customers. You might be able to speak to them directly because you have a geographic connection to them.

Use this direct connection if you can. In my job working with the giants among the hosting companies, cable, or telecommunications providers, I know direct and honest interaction with their customers is a prized commodity. We work hard to get close to their customers. Together we exert significant effort to return to a more natural and understanding customer relationship.

If you still have direct and authentic customer relationships, preserve and nurture them. You can always add the analytical tools to your arsenal as your business grows.

How to Implement the Essence of Customer Success

A successful customer success department must include key players, an organized structure, and dedication to relationship management.

Executive Buy-In Propels the Success of the CS Team

> **Well-executed CS is where value for the customer and the company intersect.**

As with all innovative or change-driven efforts, the success of the innovation is based on whether the executive team buys into the idea. A well-executed CS operation has a significant impact on the overall operation of a company. A CS team that does not have the full backing of executives will find themselves without an identity and no clear set of goals. There is nothing worse for a CS team than doing splendid work that goes unnoticed . Customer success departments can give important insights to product management and support the organization or marketing department. If a business does not listen to its CS team, it is the beginning of the end of that team.

A Fully Integrated CS Team Makes the Difference

A CS team that is integrated into the company can have a positive effect on multiple departments. Well-executed CS is where value for the customer and the company intersect. As such, it can guarantee customers receive and accept marketing messages with a positive mindset because they have a good relationship with the company.

Challenges with a product leads to constructive feedback. You only learn about these challenges when you have a mechanism in place to hear the concerns. This is invaluable intelligence for product management and development. It can also give you insights on the future needs of your customer base.

A satisfied customer looks to your brand first when she is considering an upgrade or is ready to buy a new product.

As you will see in the following examples, CS can aid marketing, customer support, and product management. The capabilities are almost limitless depending on how seriously your company takes CS.

What Kind of Customer Success Team Does Your Company Need?

Among the many different objectives of a CS team, you should address the topics most important to your company first. As you can see in Graphic XVII, there are five basic organizational models for a CS team. Which of those addresses the biggest initial need for your company? One important trait all customer success models (CSM) have in common is a "doer" mentality. The best CS teams are not reactive; they don't wait until something goes wrong. The best CS teams are proactive and address situations long before escalation is necessary. If you have the choice and you want to build a serious CS team, the mix of a hands-on executive and a complimentary manager will put you in a position to implement many of the five organizational models or profiles in a short time. From there, the executive in charge of your CSM can develop the CS operation over time.

XVII. The Five Organizational Models of Customer Success

1. FIREFIGHTER CSM

2. SALES-ORIENTED CSM

3. SERVICE-ORIENTED CSM

4. INTEGRATED CSM

5. PARTNERSHIP CSM

Why Is Relationship Management So Important?

Relationship management is at the core of what marketing wants to achieve. Customer success efforts have the same purpose. When we build relationships, we try to win new customers to our brand and convert them into loyal customers. (Davidson, R., 2011).

> Relationship management is at the core of what marketing wants to achieve.

Insightful discussions with your customer require a trusting relationship. Your company has the responsibility to create this relationship and make sure it increases intangible value for your customers. As I mentioned, the quality of the relationships you keep with your customers decides the success of your business.

The digitalization and empowerment of customers has played a significant role in the need for a strong customer success team. Consumers now measure companies against large numbers of competitors from both local and global markets. It does not matter if the company choses to play or not. It is the customers' choice if that is who they size you up against. At the same time, digitalization has made it easy for your users to look for cheaper offerings and make a quick change. Finding the better prize has become a public sport and there are portals everywhere that support that trend.

If you fight the price-dumping battle, your business will eventually become extinct. No business can succeed over the long haul this way. Sure, short-term campaigns may promise success, but you have to be careful that the low special campaign prices are not what your audience comes expect. This makes your product or service irrelevant and replaceable as soon as the next best offer comes around.

Instead, you must create value for your customers that reaches beyond pricing. This is where the relationships you create with your customers add value to your product or service. Anything and everything that enhances the relationship you have with your customers adds tangible and intangible value to the plus side when the customer evaluates if they should switch to another provider or manufacturer. The overall customer or user experience with your product and your brand is the distinguishing factor.

Managing this is a "long-term, scientifically engineered, and professionally directed strategy" (Customer Success Association, 2016).

XVIII. Ideal Customer Lifecycle Progression

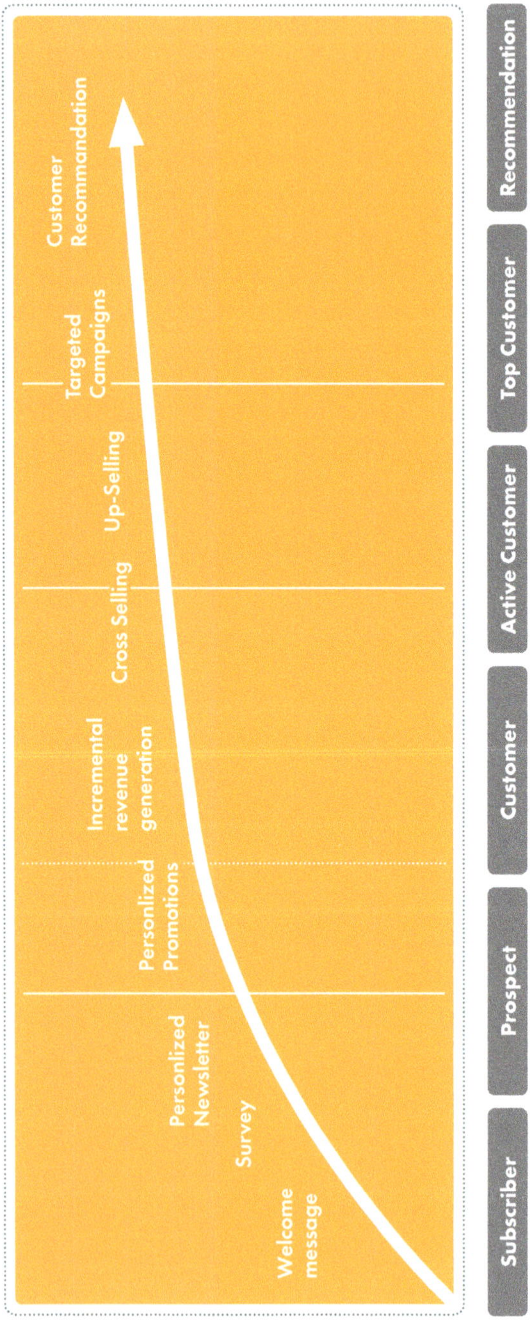
Welcome message
Survey
Personlized Newsletter
Personlized Promotions
Incremental revenue generation
Cross Selling
Up-Selling
Targeted Campaigns
Customer Recommandation
Subscriber
Prospect
Customer
Active Customer
Top Customer
Recommendation

Key take aways

To Do

NYMA

CS Should Be an Integral Part of Your Sales Operation

The easy answer to, "Why include CS in sales efforts?" is, "Because CS is your sales team's best buddy in the company." Well-executed CS ensures the customers acquired in the sales process are happy after they have started using the service or product. When customers are happy, returning sales or word-of-mouth recommendations work in your sales team's favor.

When we look a bit deeper, CS also empowers the sales process right from the start. The intelligence gathered by the CS team about the target audience, their preferences, and their "desired outcome," makes the sales process easier and allows more targeted campaigns. Feeding the prospect with the right product or service information at the right time accelerates not only the decision-making phase but also generates trust. Of course, this is all based on the premise that you feed the prospect truthful and dependable information.

Depending on your business and the product or services you offer, CS is also involved when you onboard customers or users because CS enriches the post-sale experience with free extras, guidance, and, at the right time, with up- and cross-selling opportunities for the sales team. See graphic XVIII for an illustration of the various aspects CS brings to the sales team's table.

XIX. The Different Aspects of Sales

Post-Sale enrich the experience

Streamline-sales & registration process

Offer guidance directly after registration

Define clear packages

SALES

POST-SALE GUIDANCE

Optimize the webportal experience

Offer help every step of sales process

Look & Feel state of the art

UP-/CROSS SELL

Offer packages that make sense right away

Make it easy to upgrade to other packages

Make upsell part of design!

SALES	UP-/CROSS SELL	POST-SALE GUIDANCE
Sales is not only about selling, but also about providing the customer with all the information she needs to base her decision on.	Utilize the great potential for upsell and cross-sell. 5% of premium customers buy other products.	A client that is lost, is a client that is unavailable. The best offers today create immediate and several support & guidance touch points with the customer.

How to Measure Success of the CS-Team

There are three major key performance indicators (KPIs) you can use to measure your CS team.

- Revenue (sales, revenue share, conversion rates, up- / cross-selling)
- Churn rates (reduced churn rates achieved)
- Customer satisfaction (intangible, requires active measurement)

When you ask ten different CS executives, you will receive eleven different answers about the best KPI to measure the success of their work. This is because there are many goals of CS teams, as I described. You can always put individual KPIs in place for individual members and then add intangible components you will need to measure. The intangible should be customer satisfaction, but the definition of "customer" can be misleading. A well-integrated CS team serves both internal and external customers. Depending on that mix, a 360-degree review of customer satisfaction might lead to the best results.

Growth Hacking Funnel: The Daily Business of Your Customer Success Team

Once you have your CS team in place, it is time to put the crew to work. No matter how you decide to structure your team, you must cover five key tasks. In honor of my early days at Liebfrauenschule, I call them:

"The Holy Quintet of Customer Success"

- Acquisition
- Activation
- Retention
- Recommendation
- Revenue

Although these terms are used in the internet industry, they also apply perfectly to any mom and pop business, retail store, or the mechanic garage around the corner.

Acquisition

This is the most salesy of Customer Success tasks because it lays the foundation for a successful sale. Pay attention to who takes responsibility for this task, a sales rep or a CS expert, because who takes charge of this depends heavily on your market. If you're working on a big, high-level deal in which personal relationships matter, it is likely you would not use the rather remote nature of a CS manager on the phone in a call center, on a chat, or via social media. In this instance you would to send a sales representative who can leverage relationships and cater to the customer's needs. This approach also considers the longer sales cycles for large customers, longer than a traditional CS manager usually handles.

The groundwork is much the same in both cases, tough. It requires a deep understanding of your customers' wants and needs, and excellent product or service marketing to attract the attention of a prospect.

There are many steps a Customer Success (CS) Manager or a traditional sales rep takes to build a sales funnel:

- Prospecting

  Prospecting is generating leads of potential new customers. In an ideal case, marketing supports the work of customer success and sales with infrastructure (websites, social media, campaigns) that generates leads to fill the sales funnel. This form of lead generation is ideal for products or services that are not too complex or need a large amount of customization or user education.

- Customer Contact

  In any form of outbound sales, the CS manager or sales rep must actively reach out to the prospect to close the deal. An old sales lesson tells us most sales efforts fail because the sales rep never contacted the lead. This warning is still worth heeding. A lack of follow-through in the sales cycle is one of the biggest reasons for a failed sale after the team generates a lead. It is, therefore, key to have an efficient lead-tracking system in place. You do not want to leave a sale on the table because someone did not contact a potential customer.

  For apps and products that don't need to be customized, you can cover everything I have described with a clear lead-generation and sales web page. The individual elements in this book work together as a team to create the perfect digital environment that generates leads, guides the user through prospecting and needs-analysis, provides reinforcing social proof to cover objections, and then closes the sale. Ideally, this well-designed online experience and the product itself ensures new customers are onboarded, educated, and quickly transformed into active users. The CS team then checks in during the follow-up phase to make sure the new and hopefully active customer has everything he/ she needs.

Activation

A more traditional customer success task, activation is all about getting the customer onboard (onboarding) quickly and with as little stress as possible. Customer Success teams ensure new customers use a product or services successfully right off the bat. Traditionally a concern for software companies, firms like Apple and SoulCycle have shown activation is also important for other types of businesses. Consider for a moment the set-up desks at Apple stores that invite users to have their new devices configured right there, in the store. It does not matter if a device was bought online or at another retail store, Apple understands a good first experience with their device is a crucial element to the customer's overall positive opinion of their brand. Only a properly onboarded user creates more revenue through app sales or in-app-upsells. Apple wants their customers to be active users of their devices and the ecosystem they built around them. Over the years, Apple's success has hinged on more than their devices. Their devices are mere (if very pretty) enablers of their constant and closed revenue streams that only start with the purchase and activation of the app. This trend is not going away, it appears to be on the rise.

Although a different industry, SoulCycle has a similar business model. A fitness company that offers indoor cycling classes, their entire focus is to get you on your first ride. The onboarding for that is seamless. All you really must do is show up. Do you have no shoes? No worries, you can rent them in the store. Drinks, gum, hairbands, and towels are readily available as are the trainers who set you up on your bike. After your ride, SoulCycle supplies everything you need to shower-off and tackle the rest of your day. Did you love the music that played during the class? There is a playlist. Do you want to go back and ride with the same trainer? Course schedules are presented in an easy-to-use app as are those of other trainers closer to your location. Customers can buy workout packages through the app. And they prefer it that way because it is easy. The company strives to reduce and eliminate any barriers that could keep you from coming to their classes.

Well, you still must be motivated to exercise and get there on your own.

Similar tactics work for rental car companies that pick up their customers or car dealerships that offer free courtesy cars. This business strategy is all about reducing discomfort for the customer and encouraging them to return and buy more products or services. This brings us to the next point, retention.

Retention

Winning new customers is incredibly expensive and puts a huge strain on your resources. I am not prone to hyperbole, so take my word for it, it is worth it on many levels to keep existing customers happy. And, as I have mentioned, customers talk about their experiences, especially if they didn't like it. Today's customers have more ways than ever to spread the word, and quickly too. As such, it makes double sense to do everything in your power to create a customer base who are active users of your product or take frequent advantage of your services. Those are the customers who renew their subscriptions, keep buying your product, or seek your services. Keeping a customer is much like keeping any other relationship in place. If you want to have a solid relationship with someone, you must interact with them in the right amount and make sure they are happy. When you offer customers relevant and valuable information the relationship is a benefit to them. You must be there when your customers are looking for support, or anything else for that matter. Of all things you must focus on as a businessperson, providing a high-quality experience with you and your product should be at the top of the list. Finally, ask your customers what you can do to deliver a better product or service, and then act on their feedback. If that sounds like a lot of work, try constantly winning new customers. Keeping those you have is by far the better strategy.

Recommendations

The arduous work you put in to maximize customer retention pays off when your customers do some of the sales work for you and recommend your product to their social circle. Recommendations are the ideal basis for organic growth because they multiply the reach of your original sales channels. Even better, people trust a good word about your product from friends, family, or, at the very least, other users, more than they will ever trust your sales pitch. A well-organized system to gather and help customers communicate recommendations can thus make a significant difference in the success of your company. If you own a retail business, you can encourage customers to recommend your product by offering a bonus to them and the new customer they bring along. If you are worried about bonus hunters, extend the period or the financial threshold after which you give the bonus. Although bonus hunters are a thing, I have never seen a case where it was worth limiting bonus offers to protect against the insignificant few who might take advantage of the offer. If you set it up correctly, you will always achieve break-even or better.

> Customers who bring new customers are the holy grail and ultimate prize for any business.

Customers who bring new customers are the holy grail and ultimate prize for any business.

Revenue

Nothing we have done to this point is worthwhile if it does not generate revenue for your business. That should not be a surprising or at all significant statement, but it is. I have seen a lot of founders or even proven business owners become so busy that they lose sight of this vital aspect and the primary goal of their activities: create revenue.

> **Nothing we have done to this point is worthwhile if it does not generate revenue for your business.**

Making money is the prime goal of all the steps we have laid out so far, just as it would be in any Transformers movie. If you are involved in activities in which the goal is not revenue creation, you need to reassess your priorities. Unless the business is a hobby or you are running a non-profit organization, generating revenue is always at the top of your list. If it is not, you need a new list.

However, in the context of the growth-hacking sequence of Acquisition, Activation, Retention, and Recommendation, "Revenue" focuses on generating campaigns and promotions that create revenue. Once your lead-generation activities are successful and customers stand in your store – virtual or real-life – you must make sure there are attractive offers that make them want to take the step from prospects to buying customers. For this, you need well-defined and targeted packages with proper pricing that encourages potential customers to take the last leap and make a purchase.

You should have all the necessary information and insights ready that will enable you to create the right offers. If you are unsure, you can always create a/b testing models in which you switch around your pitches. It is much easier to do this online than it is to do it in a physical retail shop because you can define different landing pages and sales skews for customers and compare the success of each. In a retail store, try various offers and promotions and see how customers react. Just because you do it one way today, does not mean you can't adjust and do it a different way tomorrow. Do not go crazy with this idea in the retail space; returning customers may wonder why they paid $5 for a pair of socks yesterday and you want them to pay $25 today or $1 tomorrow. Let common sense prevail.

A

Leave no user behind!

Customer Success for a product launch is mainly about customer care. What can you do to optimize the onboarding experience?

What and how much you know about your users is your most valuable tool. This knowledge will give you insights into who is the least and who is the most apt user/customer. Study what you know about your users/customers and figure out how to make their shopping, first use, and onboarding easy and pleasant.

Look at your point of sale; whether it is in a fashion retail store, a tire shop, or via an app online: Why did the customer come to you and how can you make sure she gets what she is looking for? How can you help her choose a product, or select the right tier if there are various price points or service levels? How can you guide your customer through this process? How much help can you offer on-demand? How soon can you get in touch with your customer, whether you approach the customer in the store (very soon) or via a pop-up chat window (soon, immediately if user is identified as active).

Post purchase, what additional support, help, or tutorials can you provide to ensure the customer stays happy with her purchase decision?

Then, depending on the product, be prepared to quickly switch from help with the old product to being in position for her next

B

Adopting a customer success mindset:

Look at every department in your company and ask the question: Do we have a customer success mindset?

Is sales enabled to sell the product in a fashion that is beneficial to both the customer and your company? A bad sale creates a negative reputation, which in turn can result in negative sales funnel progression.

Does your product have the customers' success in mind? If a product does not meet customers' expectation, it will create unhappy customers. Your product is not just one thing a customer buys from you, rather it is the basis for their holistic interaction with your company. It reflects on everything about your brand such as product marketing, sales, brand marketing, the product itself, packaging, pricing, service (trials, returns, changes), support, and customer care.

A customer success mindset starts at the top of the company and

C

First look at workstream B and then at stream A.

▶ Which of the two better applies to your situation or to your company?

▶ What are the takeaways?

▶ What are your company's customer success 5 strengths and 5 weaknesses?

▶ Do you leverage the strengths as an advantage or unique selling proposition (USP)?

▶ What can you do to mitigate the weaknesses? Who should you involve to discuss and implement improvements?

Key take aways

To Do

Summary

Going to market with a product or building your company's marketing from the ground up is not an easy task. There are many things to consider and even more steps to take. It is not rocket science, however.

Once you learn the fundamental steps, the persistence to stick with it and get it done will decide your success.

Your process will be like when I was a soldier in PsyOps. In the way I gathered information and distributed instructions about landmines and the voting process, you will go out and talk to your audience. Well, when I say talk, I mean listen. If you really listen, you will learn everything about your audience that you need to provide them with the service and product they are looking for.

Know your customers and put them at the center of your strategy.

This is also the reason I think market segmentation and personas are so important for you as marketers. Know your customers and put them at the center of your strategy. Once you get to know your clientele, you will create the plans to follow through the process, one step after the other, closer to the launch of your product. No shortcuts. Every step counts and is important for the greater good. Like building with Legos, every piece is important.

In this book I tried to equip you with the steps, the processes, and the plans you need to cover all your bases. You may not become the Steve Jobs of your industry, but it will help you find success and a solid foundation to build upon.

What comes next?

First, use all the resources noted throughout this book. Do the exercises, visit my website (nycmarketingacademy.

com) and download the templates and examples. Follow me on social media and join the groups. Lastly, at courses.nycmarketingacademy.com, you will find several video-based and self-paced courses that can further help you accomplish your goals.

Feel free to reach out. Let's use this as a start to stay connected and interact. I am interested to hear how this book helped you or what you think it is missing. Which questions did it answer for you, which did it leave open, and what new questions did it raise?

> **If you don't start and finish, you default to failure.**

Thank you for taking the time to read this book. I appreciate it and hope to hear or read from you soon.

Remember, do not stop. The biggest difference between failure and success is persistence. If you don't start and finish, you default to failure.

Have fun and success will follow!

Good luck.

✎ Key take aways

☑ To Do

-
-
-
-
-
-
-
-
-
-
-
-
-
-

NYMA

NYMA

NYMA

References

1. Reijonen, H., & Laukkanen, T. (2010). Customer relationship-oriented marketing practices in SMEs, *Marketing Intelligence & Planning*, *28*(2), 117–136. https://www.deepdyve.com/lp/emerald-publishing/customer-relationship-oriented-marketing-practices-in-smes-xR-J400AZqI?articleList=%2Fsearch%3Fquery%3Drelationships%2Bin%2Bmarketing

2. Gilmore, A., Carson D., & Grant, K (2001). SME marketing practice. *Marketing Intelligence & Planning, 19*(1), 6–11.

3. Firdaus, A., & Kanyan, A. (2012) Managing relationship marketing in the food service industry. *Marketing Intelligence & Planning, 32*(3), 293–310.
   https://www.deepdyve.com/lp/emerald-publishing/managing-relationship-marketing-in-the-food-service-industry-jugZEobltU

4. Tsimonis, G., & Dimitriadis, S. (2013). Brand strategies in social media. *Marketing Intelligence & Planning, 32*(3), 328–344.
   https://www.deepdyve.com/lp/emerald-publishing/brand-strategies-in-social-media-RdoG-CmN5Ey

5. Kaplan, A. M., & Haenlein, M. (2010). Users of the world, unite! The challenges and opportunities of social media. *Business Horizons, 53*(1), 59–68.

6. Wedel, M., & Kamakura, W. (2000). Market Segmentation: Conceptual and Methodological Foundations. *International Series in Quantitative Marketing*. Kluwer Academic Publishers.
   http://www.amazon.com/Market-Segmentation-Methodological-International-Quantitative/

dp/0792386353/ref=sr_1_1?s=books&ie=UT-F8&qid=1340106986&sr=1-1&key-words=Wedel%2C+M.%2C+%26+Kamaku-ra%2C+W.+%282000%29.+Market+Segmen-tation%3A?_encoding=UTF8&tag=segmstud-guid-20

7. Webster, F., Jr. (1984). *Industrial Marketing Strategy*. Wiley.
http://www.amazon.com/Industrial-Mar-keting-Strategy-Frederick-Webster/dp/047111989X?_encoding=UTF8&tag=segm-studguid-20

8. QuickMBA.com (2010). *Market Segmentation.*
http://www.quickmba.com/marketing/mar-ket-segmentation/

9. Payne, F. (2012). Developing superior value prop-ositions: a strategic marketing imperative. *Journal of Service Management. 25*(2). 213–227.
https://www.deepdyve.com/lp/em-erald-publishing/developing-superi-or-value-propositions-a-strategic-mar-keting-9GVhQdtSCp?articleList=/search?query=creating+a+value+proposi-tion&utm_campaign=pluginGoogleSearch&utm_source=pluginGoogleSearch&utm_medi-um=plugin

10. Camlek, V. (2010). How to spot a real value prop-osition. *Information Services & Use. 30*(3–4), 119–123.
https://www.deepdyve.com/lp/ios-press/how-to-spot-a-real-value-proposition-z0uTRWm-BcB?articleList=/search?query=creating+a+val-ue+proposition&utm_campaign=pluginGoogle-

Search&utm_source=pluginGoogleSearch&utm_medium=plugin

11. Laja, P. (2012). Useful Value Proposition Examples (and How to Create a Good One). http://conversionxl.com/value-proposition-examples-how-to-create/#

12. Human Resource Management International. (2013) Social networking gets serious Social networking moves beyond timewasting to become a powerful business tool. *Human Resource Management International Digest. 21*(3). https://www.deepdyve.com/lp/emerald-publishing/social-networking-gets-serious-social-networking-moves-beyond-iAzme9ugBX?articleList=%2Fsearch%3Fquery%3Dlinkedin%2Bmarketing%2Bstrategy%26page%3D2

13. Boosenger, A. (2014). 3 Ways Any Business Can Market on Pinterest. http://www.socialmediaexaminer.com/3-ways-to-market-on-pinterest/#more-63076

14. Chari, S., Christodoulides, G., Presi, C., Wenhold, J., & Casaletto, J.P. (2016). Consumer Trust in User-Generated Brand Recommendations on Facebook. *Psychology & Marketing, 33*(12), 1071–108. https://www.deepdyve.com/lp/wiley/consumer-trust-in-user-generated-brand-recommendations-on-facebook-e7VqBAkmqy

15. L. Murphy, & A. McClafferty. (2016). Customer Success: The Best Kept Secret of Hyper-Growth Startups. http://www.forbes.com/sites/alexmcclafferty/2015/05/18/customer-success/#6ee884463144

16. Customer Success Association. (2016). The Definition of Customer Success.
http://www.customersuccessassociation.com/definition-customer-success-management/

17. Metha, N. (2016). The essential guide to customer success.
http://www.gainsight.com/guides/the-essential-guide-to-customer-success/

18. What is Customer Success
http://www.bluenose.com/blog/what-is-customer-success/

19. Bullas, J. (2016). 9 Ways to Grow Your Startup with Social Media. http://www.jeffbullas.com/2016/03/31/9-ways-grow-your-startup-with-social-media/

20. Davidson, R. (2011). Web 2.0 as a marketing tool for conference centers. *International Journal of Event and Festival Management, 2*(2), 117–138. https://www.deepdyve.com/lp/emerald-publishing/web-2-0-as-a-marketing-tool-for-conference-centres-ZboWfy54cd

21. Mashable. (2016). 7 worthwhile ways to automate social media. http://mashable.com/2016/02/01/automate-social-media/#s9QjDWsbAPqP

22. Cleary, I. (2016). 7 Terrific Time Saving Social Media Automation Tools that you have to use! *RazorSocial.*
http://www.razorsocial.com/social-media-automation/

23. Nielsen, L., & Storgaard Hansen, K. (2014). Personas is applicable – A Study on the use of Personas In Denmark. Association for Computing Machinery. https://www.deepdyve.com/lp/association-for-computing-machinery/personas-is-applicable-a-study-on-the-use-of-perso-

nas-in-denmark-WtLmhFVPVH?articleList=%2F-
search%3Fquery%3Dpersonas%26page%3D2

24. Kitchen, P.J., & Burgmann, I. (2015). Integrated marketing Communication: making it work on a strategic
level. *Journal of Business Strategy, 36*(4), 34–39.
https://www.deepdyve.com/lp/emerald-publish-
ing/integrated-marketing-communication-mak-
ing-it-work-at-a-strategic-level-wJc3m0WvzO?arti-
cleList=%2Fsearch%3Fquery%3DMarketing%2BCom-
munication%2BStrategy%26page%3D2

25. Skok, D. (2016). Managing Customer Success to Reduce Churn.
http://www.forentrepreneurs.com/customer-success/

26. Chargify, N. A. (2016). SaaS Customer Success: the
secret to reducing churn and increasing MRR.
https://www.chargify.com/blog/saas-customer-success/

27. McClafferty, A., & Murphy, L. (2015). Costumer Success: The best kept secret of hyper-growth startups.
http://www.forbes.com/sites/alexmcclaf-
ferty/2015/05/18/customer-success/2/#240b3f467fb3

28. Customer Success Association. (2016). The Definition of
Customer Success.
http://www.customersuccessassociation.com/defini-
tion-customer-success-management/

29. Social Media Statistics.
https://www.statista.com/statistics/272014/glob-
al-social-networks-ranked-by-number-of-users/

30. Read All About It! The Eight Elements of News.
https://www.progress.com/blogs/read-all-about-
it!-the-eight-elements-of-news

31. https://insights.newscred.com/content-marketing-best-practices-from-top-brands/

32. https://www.spredfast.com/social-marketing-blog/seo-and-content-best-practices-2017

33. http://contentmarketinginstitute.com/2016/08/content-marketing-trends/

34. Boyarsky, K. 10 Simple Ways to Optimize Your Website for Lead Generation. https://blog.hubspot.com/marketing/optimize-website-for-lead-generation

35. Crestodina, A. Lead Generation: Website Best Practices. https://www.orbitmedia.com/blog/lead-generation-website-practices/

36. The Ten Commandments of an Awesome Lead-Generating Website. https://blog.kissmetrics.com/lead-generating-website/

37. Krug, S. (2005). Don't Make Me Think. New Riders Publishing.

38. Hatfield, T. (2018). Top 7 Biggest Content Marketing Mistakes. https://www.inturact.com/blog/top-7-biggest-content-marketing-mistakes

Index

After page reference: "f" means "figure," "t" means "table."